Jack's Handy Guide To Trusts
Staying Out of Court

by
Jack Forbes

Jack's Handy Guide To Trusts
Staying Out of Court

by
Jack Forbes

Copyright ©2017 by Jack Forbes

ISBN 978-0-9836418-8-9

Published by
JAFO PUBLISHING
375 Redondo Avenue
PMB 320
Long Beach, California 90814

Printed in the United States of America

Book Design—Typography—Cover Design—Retouching
M. Redmond—Redmond & Associates
marioncreative@gmail.com

Contact Information:
www.JafoPublishing.com

PREFACE

A trust document, whether a revocable or irrevocable trust, places property "into" the trust and gives instructions to the "trustee" as to how to manage, control and distribute the "corpus" (principal) of the trust and the income, if any, of the trust. For every trust, there must be a trustee and eventually that trustee or a "successor" (subsequent) trustee is saddled with certain legal duties **of a fiduciary**—that is, a person holding a position of trust and confidence with certain fiduciary duties to both the trust and (at some point) to all beneficiaries of the trust. Those legal duties, owed by the trustee, are created either by law (statutory law and "case" law from published/"citable" precedent appellate cases) or by the terms and conditions of the trust instrument itself.

Therein lies the problem, for once the trustor or "settlor" (the person or whose property was placed in the trust and who otherwise caused the trust to be drawn up) has passed away or has become incompetent, the person accepting responsibility to be the trustee *must* comply with the fiduciary responsibilities pertaining to the "administration" (*meaning*, execution of the trust's purposes, following the law and the trust terms and conditions) pertaining to and of the trust. Let's just say, to be congenial, "*Easier said than done.*" The disputes which have resulted in published case law judicial "Opinions" (decisions) are *legion* regarding trustees who have found themselves in *expensive and time-consuming litigation* over issues of whether they properly discharged their respective trustee responsibilities. And for these trustees, the actual or perceived mistakes and breaches of trust duties *may lead both to costly litigation expense and extensive personal liability.*

So, what are the fiduciary responsibilities of trustees in California, and how can even a layman (someone with virtually no experience in the administration of trusts) *reliably approach* and *fairly satisfy* their responsibilities in a new-found capacity as trustee of a trust? Since the trust was probably created at least in part with the idea of keeping the trust assets *out of Probate Court*, what steps can the trustee take to minimize the chances of ending up there anyway?

Jack's Handy Guide To Trusts—Staying Out of Court is a book designed to help a trustee of a trust, governed by California law, to properly discharge his or her fiduciary duties and, in the process, to minimize exposure to and the likelihood of costly litigation. The book is not, however, a substitute for competent legal advice specific to the particular trust instrument with which you, or the trustee, may be dealing.[1] Optimally, a trustee should seek independent legal advice from a competent attorney in the field of Wills and Trusts to guide them through the maze pertaining to the administration of trusts governed by California law.

However, if you elect to refrain from consulting legal counsel or simply wish to have a *personal understanding* of the basics of California trust administration, then this book is for you.

Jack Forbes
Author

[1] **Important Disclaimer**: This work is not intended to offer legal advice pertaining to any particular trust instrument, nor as to how a Trustee should or should not administer any particular trust, and should not be relied upon as a substitute for the reader retaining his own independent counsel for legal advice which is specific to the particular trust involved and the particular legal jurisdiction governing the administration of the trust when a legal issue arises. Moreover, statutory law can change from time to time in any jurisdiction, including California, judicial opinions may be modified, superseded or overruled and new judicial opinions may arise which materially affect the law pertaining to trusts, and this book may not take such changes into account. Also, any of the various hypothetical scenarios set forth herein are fictional and are not intended to depict actual events which may have occurred. Any similarity to any actual events or persons referred to herein is unintended and merely coincidental.

ENDORSEMENT

ack's Handy Guide To Trusts—*Staying Out of Court*
is a must read for anyone creating a California
living trust, nominated as a trustee of a living trust
or designated as a beneficiary of a living trust.
A decisively sharp California trust litigation attorney,
Jack Forbes lays it on the line to help readers navigate
the treacherous waters of living trusts and stay out
of court whenever feasible.

Dale A. Martin, Esq., J.D.
Lecturer, Law
California State University at Fullerton

DEDICATION

This book is dedicated to all those trusting and perhaps misguided persons who have instilled their faith in utilizing *inter vivos* trusts instead of relying upon the Probate Courts to supervise the Administration of their Estates.

With Probate Court administration, you have the benefit of an experienced judicial officer (Superior Court Judge) and his staff of specialized professionals, including the Probate Attorney, overseeing the moves and filings of the executor or executrix of a Will or the trustee of a testamentary trust, including the usual requirement of posting of a bond to insure the proper discharge of those duties.

With an *inter vivos* trust, you have only a professional trustee, or a layman who more than likely is way over his or her head, who attempts to discharge its, his or her fiduciary duties. The result is often expensive chaos, and a profound misuse and waste of trust assets.

Jack Forbes

TABLE OF CONTENTS

TABLE OF CONTENTS

Jack's Handy Guide To Trusts

Staying Out of Court

CHAPTER 1
The Legal Basics of a Trust

Legal Framework of a Trust

California law pertaining to the administration of trusts is largely statutory. *See, e.g.,* California Probate Code[2] Section 15642 (grounds for removal of trustee); Section 15687 (limitations on trustee compensation for legal services); Section 16060 (duty to inform); Section 16061 (duty to report); Section 16061.5 (duty to provide terms of trust); Section 16061.7 (duty to provide notice); Section 16062 (duty to account); and Section 16461 (limitations on certain categories of potential trustee liability). Judicial opinion from California courts, however, also plays a major role in shaping the duties and liabilities pertaining to the administration of trusts.

A "trust" is an arrangement where property of some nature is transferred, or intended to be transferred, by the trustor to a trust (a legal embodiment) with the intent that it be held, managed, and distributed

---

[2] All references to a "Code", unless otherwise specified, are to the California statutory law. For example, "Probate Code" would mean the California Probate Code.

by the "trustee" for the benefit of one or more beneficiaries. *Presta v. Tepper* (2009) 179 Cal.App.4ᵗʰ 909[3]; *Askew v. Resource Funding Ltd.* (1979) 94 Cal. App.3d 402; *Raffo v. Foltz (*1930) 106 Cal.App. 51. A trustor is also sometimes referred to as the *settlor.* The *trustee* holds and controls the property, which is an asset of the trust, for the interest of the *beneficiary. Fiduciary duties* arise from a trust whereby the trustee must abide by certain fiduciary and equitable duties respecting the trust property. *Hobbs v. Buck* (1981) 115 Cal.App.3d 176. As a fiduciary, a trustee is required to act with the *highest of good faith towards the beneficiary, with full disclosure of material facts.* A "trustee" includes an original, additional or successor trustee, whether or not appointed or confirmed by a court. Probate Code Section 84.

This book concerns trusts which are in the first instance typically administered extra-judicially, as opposed to trusts which require, by their terms or operation, judicial oversight in their administration or enforcement. Also, this book concerns "active," as oppose to "dry," trusts. An active trust is where a trustee has a duty to manage the trust property [*In re Shaw's* Estate (1926) 198 Cal. 352; *Gray v. Union Trust*

---

[3] The case citations that you see in this book are legal shorthand for lengthier book titles. For example, the citation 341 So.2d 261 would mean volume 341 of Southern Reports, Second Edition, at the starting page of 261. The shorthand version of case citations, including the name of the case, is how the case may be located and read in full on the internet, through on-line legal research systems such as WestLaw or Lexis, or at any well-stocked Law Library.

Co. of San Francisco (1915) 171 Cal. 637], preserve it [*Wood v. American Nat. Bank* (1932) 125 Cal.App. 125], sell and convey the property and delegate the proceeds according to the terms of the trust [*Craven v. Dominguez Estate Co.* (1925) 72 Cal.App.713; *Withers v. Bonsfield* (1919) 42 Cal.App. 304], re-convey the property [*Withers, supra*], or distribute and allocate the property according to the terms of the trust upon the settlor's death [*Gray, supra*].

In a dry trust, the *beneficiary* may enforce actual possession and enjoyment of the trust property and has absolute control over their beneficial use, possession and enjoyment of the property, as well as a right to call for legal title thereto. *Ringrose v. Gleadall* (1911) 17 Cal.App. 664.

"Acceptance" by a Nominated Trustee

Neither notice to a trustee nor his acceptance is required to *create* a valid trust. However, before any duties of the trust are imposed upon him, a trustee must in some legally recognizable manner *accept* the appointment as trustee. A trustee may accept his duties as trustee by signing either the trust instrument or a separate written acceptance [Probate Code Section 15600(a)(1)], or, by "knowingly exercising powers or performing duties under the trust instrument." Probate Code Section 15600(a)(2).

Thereafter,

> "On acceptance of the trust, the trustee

has a duty to administer the trust according to the trust instrument and, except to the extent the trust instrument provides otherwise, according to this division." Probate Code Section 16000.

Acceptance or declination (declining the appointment from the trust) by a trustee is a crucial step in determining the rights and obligations of a prospective trustee. Acceptance of the trust is necessary to make a person subject to the duties and privileges of a trustee. Probate Code Sections 15000-19403; *Smith v. Bliss* (1941) 44 Cal.App.2d 171.

Scenario: A trust appoints Joe as the successor trustee (once the trustor, who is the original trustee, dies) and requires him to administer a portfolio of stocks and bonds as well as a savings and checking account for the benefit of two minor children of the trustor. Joe has been placed as a signatory onto the trust checking account. The trust refers to Probate Code section 15600 and requests that the trustee sign a document agreeing to become the successor trustee. The trustor dies but Joe refuses to sign the successor trustee acceptance document. Nevertheless, he proceeds to write checks for the benefit of the two minor children for two years. In that period of time, the stocks steadily decline in value and no accounting is prepared. The minors eventually hire an attorney and sue for an accounting and for losses to the stock portfolio. Joe defends on the ground that he never accepted responsibility as the successor trustee.

Analysis: Formal written acceptance of the responsibilities of appointment as a trustee is not necessary when the person knowingly exercises the powers and authority of the position by performing duties and responsibilities pursuant to the trust. In this case, for two years Joe wrote checks for the benefit of the minor children, but failed to properly manage the stock portfolio, leading to losses. He failed to render annual accountings to the beneficiaries. The Court will hold Joe personally responsible for the losses to the stock portfolio and will order him to create accountings for the two years of his administration of the trust. For violation of his fiduciary duties to the trust and to the beneficiaries of the trust, the Court may remove Joe as the successor trustee and appoint someone else. Furthermore, since the burden is upon a trustee, and not the beneficiaries, to substantiate the disposition of trust property, Joe would be held *personally liable* for any missing or otherwise un-accounted for trust assets if his accounting to the court is deficient in adequately accounting for the existence and disposition of trust assets.

Essential Elements of a Trust

An express trust, to be enforceable, must embody *five elements*: (1) a competent trustor; (2) trust intent (Probate Code Section 15201); (3) trust property (Probate Code Section 15202); (4) trust purpose (Probate Code Section 15203, 15204); and, (5) one or more beneficiaries (Probate Code Section 15205). *Luna v. Brownell* (2010) 185 Cal.App.4th 668; *Keitel v. Heubel* (2002) 103 Cal.App.4th 324.

Notwithstanding the foregoing, however, a trust designed *to defraud* creditors or others is unlawful and unenforceable. *In re Marriage of Dick* (1993) 15 Cal. App.4th 144. Also, certain donative transfers in a trust to particular categories of beneficiaries are prohibited or presumptively proscribed, such as designation of the person who drafted the instrument as being a beneficiary, or designation of a care custodian of a dependent adult who is the transferor/trustor. *See*, Probate Code Sections 21350-21351.

If a trustee is not named, an otherwise valid trust is still considered to have been created since the identity of the trustee is *not* an essential element of a valid and enforceable trust. The court will simply appoint an appropriate trustee. Probate Code Section 15660.

> **Scenario:** In Abe's Last Will & Testament, written at a time when Abe was unquestionably competent, he bequeathed his entire estate to his son, Jim, "to be turned over to him" at age 25, but "until then the estate to be handled by the executors of this will." The will further provided that prior to age 25, Jim was to be paid, "as much per month as they deem advisable." Upon Abe's death, Jim, 18 years old, claimed a right to immediately receive the entire estate and he contested that an express testamentary trust had been created which would result in a delay in that transfer until he turned 25.

> **Analysis**: All of the five essential elements for a valid trust (in this case, a "testamentary trust") had been established here: trustor competency, trust intent, trust property, trust purpose and beneficiary. The trust property was Abe's entire estate. The fact that individual items within the trust property were not specifically identified was inconsequential. The trust intent, trust purpose and beneficiary were clear: to provide for Jim until he

reached 25 years of age and then to turn over the balance of the estate to him. The trust would be enforced and a trustee appointed by the court. *Estate of Faris* (1949) 89 Cal.App.2d 515.

Trust intent must be expressed in terms of *obligatory duties* of a trustee, not merely a trustor's hope, recommendation, desire or appeal to the trustee's moral obligation. *Estate of Mitchell* (1911) 160 Cal. 618, 621; *Estate of Moore* (1967) 253 Cal.App.2d 945, 949. A different result obtains where the precatory words are directed to an executor of a will, in which case they are likely to be construed as establishing a command rather than a mere moral suggestion. *Estate of Pforr* (1904) 144 Cal. 121, 128.

Scenario: An instrument by Sam intending to create an immediate "living" trust provides, "It is my fondest hope and heartfelt desire that the trustee named in this trust use the trust property for the best interests of my beloved adult son, Terrence, in accordance with the recommendations set forth herein—to wit: for Terrence's education and welfare until he reaches age 35." Bill and Sarah, Sam's other two adult children, were the beneficiaries of the entirety of the residue of Sam's estate, and in a lawsuit, they claimed the right to an immediate probate distribution of Sam's estate.

Analysis: Here, it would seem that the living trust intent is obvious since Sam even refers to the instrument as being "this trust" and since he specifically refers to the *trustee*. But appearances can be deceiving since Sam neglected to make the duties of the trustee *imperative* in the sense of a legal obligation. Instead, Sam couched the trust duties in terms of the settlor's "fondest hope and heartfelt desire" and thus doomed the instrument to create...*nothing*. The trust never legally arose since a trustor must express an intention to impose *legally enforceable duties* upon a trustee and not merely a moral obligation of some sort. Had Sam's directive been as part of his will, however, to take effect only upon his death (i.e., a "testamentary trust"), a Probate Court would likely have construed the directives to create a *command to the executor* rather than merely a moral suggestion. In the facts of *this* case, however, involving an attempted but failed *inter vivos* trust, Bill and Sarah would be entitled to the entire estate.

The *purpose* of the trust must be adequately described so as to be enforceable by a court. A conveyance of all of a trustor's property to William, in trust for the trustor's "lodge," "[t]to have and to hold unto said trustee, his successors and assigns" does not create a trust, since there is neither a statement of a trust purpose nor a statement of the requisite manner of performance. *Wittfield v. Forster* (1899) 124 Cal. 418. Moreover, the beneficiaries must be described with such specificity as to be reasonably ascertainable as a person or class of persons. Probate Code Section 15205(b)(1).

Even where the trust assets are not actually conveyed to or into the trust itself, the trust may still be enforceable. A court may order transfer of the property to the trust upon the death or incapacity of the settler, if the trust otherwise was effectively created. *Estate of Heggstad* (1993) 16 Cal.App.4th 943.

Beneficiary's Legal Remedy

Generally, a beneficiary of a trust has three (3) years from the date of receipt of an accounting (an accounting which would place him on actual or constructive notice of a claim against the trustee), or from other actual or constructive discovery of the claim, with or without an accounting, within which to file an action. The *duty of inquiry* is triggered when there is sufficient information, through an accounting or otherwise, to put the beneficiary on reasonable notice to take action. Probate Code Section 16460; *Britton v. Girardi* 2015 WL 1519759 (Cal.App.2d Dist. 2015). A trustee is personally liable for obligations arising from ownership or control of trust property if the trustee's conduct is proved to have been intentional or negligent. Probate Code Section 18001; *Stine v. Dell'Osso* 2014 EWL 5293521 (Cal.App. 1st Dist. 2014).

Trustee Compensation and Allowance of Expenses

Compensation to a trustee, if not specified as to method of calculation in the trust instrument, is determined by reference to such factors as follows: income of the trust, success or failure of the trustee's administration, any unusual skill or experience the trustee may have brought to his work, fidelity or disloyalty, time consumed in carrying out the trust, the custom in the community, whether the work done was routine or involved skill and judgment, and any estimate the trustee has made of the value of his services. 60 CalJur3d Trusts Sect. 267, pp. 351-352; *In re McLaughlin's Estate* (1954) 43 Cal.2d 462; *Estate of Nazro* (1971) 15 Cal.App.3d 218.

An allowance of just and reasonable compensation for a Trustee's services rests in the sound discretion of the trial court, whose ruling will not be disturbed on appeal in the absence of a manifest showing of abuse. Probate Code Section 1122; *In re McLaughlin's Estate* (1954) 43 Cal.2d 462. In this regard, the trial court has wide discretion in determining and allowance of a trustee's fees. *McLaughlin's Estate, above.*

The trial court may disallow ordinary and extra-ordinary compensation expenses and attorney fees of a trustee to the extent that compensation was sought for services in connection with negligently administered trust assets. *Estate of Gump* (1991) 1 Cal.App.4th 582. In the absence of a trust provision to the contrary, a trustee is entitled to reimbursement for all expenses actually and properly incurred in the performance of the trust and reasonable compensation for his services as trustee. Civil Code Sections 2273, 2274; *Petherbridge v. Prudential Sav. & Loan Assn.* (1978) 79 Cal.App.3d 509. However, a trustee *under a trust which does not expressly provide for compensation* for the trustee's services is not entitled to any unless and until the same has been expressly approved and allowed in a judicial proceeding by the trial court. *People v. Williams.* (1956) 145 Cal.App.2d 163.

> **Scenario:** Trustee Giselle is trustee of a trust for the benefit of Charity Johnson, who was 13 at the time that the trust becomes irrevocable upon the death of Charity's parents. The trust requires Giselle to make such payments in her reasonable discretion for the "health, education and welfare" of Charity Johnson until Charity reaches 18 years of age and then to pay the entire trust balance over to Charity Johnson. The trust further provides that Giselle is to make payments first from the income of the trust, and then, if that is not adequate to provide for Charity, from the principal. Over a period of three years, Giselle periodically doles out money from the trust, fails to account and keeps

minimal receipts. Giselle fails to invest any of the $1,325,720.17 in beginning cash assets but regularly pays herself $500.00 each and every month as "trustee's fees." Charity's Guardian *ad litem* files suit against Giselle personally and against the trust claiming Giselle has breached her fiduciary duties as trustee by failing to properly expend trust money for Charity Johnson, for failing to invest the cash assets, for failing to provide annual accountings and for paying herself unreasonable compensation. The suit asks that Giselle be replaced by the court as trustee, that Giselle be ordered to provide annual accountings since the effective date of the trust, that Giselle disgorge all of the compensation she has paid to herself from trust assets and that Giselle be held personally liable in damages for failing to properly invest trust assets.

Analysis: As we will see elsewhere, this trustee has clearly breached her fiduciary duties to the beneficiary. She has failed to account at least annually as required by California statutory law. She has failed to invest the cash so as to make the cash assets work and create income for the trust. She may or may not have

Jack's Handy Guide To Trusts

paid adequate money for the health, education and welfare of Charity, since the facts are not clear in this regard. She has kept "minimal receipts" yet has a *legal duty and burden* to provide adequate substantiation that each and every expenditure charged to the trust was actually for the benefit of the trust. Giselle has apparently paid herself a "flat fee" every month of $500.00 without regard to the work spent by her as trustee in any given month. A trustee is entitled to compensation, but only based upon the pertinent factors of, *inter alia*, experience, effectiveness and benefit to the trust. In this case, Giselle failed to adequately discharge her duties to the trust and has provided no detail of her actual work each month as trustee, nor as to a reasonable hourly rate for these services. A court is likely to Order Giselle to disgorge some or all of the $500.00 per month trustee fees. The court would order Giselle to provide a proper accounting for each of the years in which she was trustee. The court would undoubtedly replace Giselle with a new trustee and would also give judgment against Giselle and in favor of the trust, for lost income due to Giselle's failure to properly invest all of the cash except for that amount reasonably necessary for normal administration of trust purposes.

CHAPTER 2
A Trustee's Duties

trustee must look to the trust instrument, and to the trust instrument alone, to determine the terms and meaning of a trust. *Shipley v. Jordan* (1929) 206 Cal. 439; *Kaiser v. Gibson* (1968) 264 Cal.App.2d 319. On the other hand, a trustee must refuse to comply with any term of the trust which is contrary to public policy. *See*, Probate Code Section 15203 (illegal trust purpose).

In the fiduciary relationship of a trustee to a trust, the trustee's sole objective must be to safeguard the interests of each of the beneficiaries. *Moeller v. Superior Court* (1997) 16 Cal.4th 1124, 1134. A failure to satisfy any fiduciary duty owed to a beneficiary may result in a breach of trust and potential personal liability of the trustee to the beneficiaries. Probate Code Section 16400.

Importantly, the standard of care owed by a trustee in the discharge of his or her fiduciary duties is not static across the board for all persons acting in the capacity of a trustee. Instead, a trustee's standard of care *varies* according to the particular level of experience and expertise which a given trustee brings to their administration of the trust. Accordingly, expert trustees must meet a *higher standard of care* than non-expert trustees. Probate Code Sections 16014 and 16040(a).

A trustee must use at least that degree of care and diligence that an ordinarily prudent person would use in connection with the particular transaction in the management of his or her own affairs. *In re Whitney's Estate* (1926) 78 Cal.App. 638. The Court in *In re Estate of Cairns* (2010) 188 Cal.App.4th 937 summarizes the duties of a trustee to include,

> "'...the duty of loyalty, the duty to avoid conflicts of interest, the duty to preserve trust property, the duty to make trust property productive, the duty to dispose of improper investments, and the duty to report and account.' (*City of Atascadero v. Merrill Lynch Pierce, Fenner and Smith, Inc.* (1998) 68 Cal.App.4th 445, 462...' Any violation of such duties constitutes a fraud against the beneficiaries. ...'" (188 Cal.App.4th at 949).

The Probate Code also describes the statutory standard of care for trustees:

> "(a) The trustee shall administer the trust with reasonable care, skill, and caution under the circumstances then prevailing

that a prudent person acting in a like capacity would use in the conduct of an enterprise of the character and with the aims to accomplish the purposes of the trust as determined from the trust instrument.

(b) The settlor may expand or restrict the standard provided in subdivision (a) by express provisions in the trust instrument. A trustee is not liable to a beneficiary for the trustee's good faith reliance on these express provisions. ..." Probate Code Sect. 16040

Probate Code Section 16014 further provides that,

"(a) The trustee has a duty to apply the full extent of the trustee's skills. ..."

A trustee may not delegate to others the performance of acts which the trustee can reasonably be required personally to perform. Probate Code Sect. 16012(a). A "trustee has a duty to take reasonable steps under the circumstances to take and keep control of and to preserve the trust property." Probate Code Sect. 16006. A "trustee has a duty to make the trust property productive under the circumstances and in furtherance of the purposes of the trust." Probate Code Sect. 16007.

A trustee must invest and manage trust assets as a prudent investor would, by considering the purposes, terms, distribution requirements, and other circumstances of the trust. In satisfying this standard, the trustee must exercise reasonable care, skill and caution. 60 CalJur3d Trusts Sect. 156, pp. 224-225; *Allen v. Hussey* (1950) 101 Cal.App.2d 457.

If a trustee delays for an unreasonable period of time before making investments, he commits a breach of the trust. *Uzyel v. Kadisha* (2010) 188 Cal. App.5th 866; *Lynch v. John M. Redfield Foundation* (1970) 9 Cal.App.3d 293. A failure to properly invest trust moneys according to the statute regarding permissible investments [Probate Code Section 16042] renders the trustee liable for interest thereon. Probate Code Sections 16440 and 16441; *In re Prior's Estate* (1952) 111 Cal.App.2d 464. A trustee who violates his duties to beneficiaries may be liable to the beneficiaries for a breach of the trust. Probate Code Sections 16400-16403.

A trustee must deal impartially as to each beneficiary so as to not treat one more preferentially than any other. *Penny v. Wilson* (2004) 123 Cal. App.4th 596, 603. The trustee must act impartially when there are multiple beneficiaries:

> "If a trust has two or more beneficiaries, the trustee has a duty to deal impartially with them and shall act impartially in investing and managing the trust property, taking into account any differing interests

of the beneficiaries." Probate Code Sect. 16047(a).

In this regard, "(a) The trustee has a duty to administer the trust solely in the interest of the beneficiaries. ..." Probate Code Sect. 16002(a). No beneficiary has a right to have a particular person selected as the Trustee and no Trustee can properly act for only some beneficiaries. He must represent all of them or he cannot properly represent any of them. *Bowles v. Superior Court of City and County of San Francisco* (1955) 44 Cal.2d 574. A Trustee must be capable and impartial and willing to faithfully execute the trust in accordance with its terms. These interests are common to all beneficiaries. *Bowles, above.*

> **Scenario:** A trust appoints Jill as successor trustee upon the death of trustor/trustee, for the benefit of a beneficiary child. The trust states that Jill is to invest the trust property, in her sound discretion, in a productive array of stocks and municipal bonds. Jill has no experience in such investments and despite her efforts, her investment yields fall 25% below the average mutual fund profits for the first year. The minor hires an attorney and sues the trustee for breach of fiduciary duty in making the trust property productive.

Analysis: Although Jill may have hired a professional stocks and bonds portfolio manager, the trust expressly allowed Jill to invest trust property, in her sound discretion, in stocks and municipal bonds. Although a professional trustee would be held to a higher standard and although the yield for Jill's investments was 25% below what professionals may have averaged in annual yield, this is probably within the standard of care for a non-professional trustee who is not otherwise an expert in managing a portfolio of stocks and bonds. Had Jill's efforts been even more unsuccessful, and over a longer period of time, the argument of incompetence *strengthens* in favor of a finding of breach of fiduciary duty and could result in personal liability of a trustee to the trust and to its beneficiaries.

Within the general administration of a trust is the responsibility of a trustee to satisfy (i.e., to pay) creditors which have established judgments[4] against the decedent trustee. In fact, a judgment against such a decedent trustee is a valid and legally enforceable

---

[4] A "judgment" in a legal sense is a final decree of a court of competent jurisdiction which is legally enforceable [unless enforcement of the judgment is "stayed" (postponed in legal effect) by statute or court ruling] against the party against whom/which the judgment is entered.

claim against both the decedent's probate estate and, if the assets of the probate estate are insufficient to satisfy the judgment, against the assets of an *inter vivos* trust which was revocable during the settlor's lifetime. *Dobler v. Arluk Medical Center Industrial Group, Inc.* (2001) 89 Cal.App.4th 530.

CHAPTER 3
Trust Accountings

ccountings as to trusts are mandated by California statutory law:

> "(a) Except as otherwise provided in this section and in Section 16064, the trustee *shall account at least annually*, at the termination of the trust, and upon a change of trustee, to each beneficiary to whom income or principal is required or authorized in the trustee's discretion to be currently distributed. ..." Probate Code Sect. 16062 (italics added for emphasis).

Content of a Proper Accounting

The requisite *contents* of a trust accounting are also established by California statute:

> "(a) An account furnished pursuant to Section 16062 shall contain the following information:
>
> > (1) A statement of receipts and disbursements of principal and income that

have occurred during the last complete fiscal year of the trust or since the last account.

(2) A statement of the assets and liabilities of the trust as of the end of the last complete fiscal year of the trust or as of the end of the period covered by the account.

(3) The trustee's compensation for the last complete fiscal year of the trust or since the last account.

(4) The agents hired by the trustee, their relationship to the trustee, if any, and their compensation, for the last complete fiscal year of the trust or since the last account.

(5) A statement that the recipient of the account may petition the court pursuant to Section 17200 to obtain a court review of the account and of the acts of the trustee.

(6) A statement that claims against the trustee for breach of trust may not be made after the expiration of three years from the date the beneficiary receives an account or report disclosing facts giving rise to the claim. ..." Probate Code Sect. 16063.

Chapter 3
Trust Accountings

Of course, a trustee need not render an accounting where the trustee and sole beneficiary are the same person. Probate Code Section 16069(b). Similarly, a trustee may be absolved from a duty to account to a beneficiary with a waiver in writing from that beneficiary [Probate Code Section 16064(b)], although certain waivers are deemed void as against public policy. Probate Code Section 16068.

The duty to account is a continuing one, so long as the trust remains in effect. *In re DeLavenga's Estate* (1958) 50 Cal.2d 480; *Knapp v. Knapp* (1940) 15 Cal.2d 237. A trustee must keep full and accurate accounts of his transactions [*Purdy v. Johnson* (1917) 174 Cal. 521].[5] The trustee is chargeable with the whole of the estate committed to his hands. [*McAdoo v. Sayre* (1904) 145 Cal. 344], and must account for all moneys received and disbursed. [*In re Evans' Estate* (1944) 62 Cal.App.2d 249]

The period expressed in a trust instrument for a beneficiary *to object* to an accounting may not be less than 180 days, absent compliance with the detailed notice provisions of Probate Code Sect. 16461.

In dealing with beneficiaries, the burden is upon the trustee to show that the beneficiary was fully informed of his or her rights and was not misled by

---

[5] The full, California Supreme Court Opinion in *Purdy v. Johnson* is reproduced in the Addendum to this book.

even an unintentional misrepresentation. *Wingerter v. Wingerter* (1886) 71 Cal. 105. The trustee has a duty of full disclosure to the beneficiaries of facts that materially affect the rights of the parties. *Bennett v. Hibernia Bank* (1956) 47 Cal.2d 540; *Ball v. Posey* (1986) 176 Cal.App.3d 1209.

Interaction with a Trust "No Contest" Clause

A beneficiary's request for information reasonably necessary to enable beneficiaries to enforce their rights in a trust is not a "contest" of the trust. Moreover, a petition to enforce a trustee's duty is neither a direct nor indirect challenge to the validity of the trust or its terms. Similarly, a pleading to compel an accounting or report of a fiduciary is not a contest. *Salter v. Lerner* (2009) 176 Cal.App.4th 1184.

Probate Code Section 21300 provides that:

> "(a) A no contest clause shall **only be enforced against the following types of contests**:
>
> > (1) A direct contest that is brought without probable cause.
> >
> > (2) A pleading to challenge a transfer of property on the grounds that it was not the transferor's property at the time of the transfer. ...
> >
> > (3) The filing of a creditor's claim or prosecution of an action based on it.

(b) For the purposes of this section, probable cause exists if, at the time of filing a contest, the facts known to the contestant would cause a reasonable person to believe that there is a reasonable likelihood that the requested relief will be granted after an opportunity for further investigation or discovery." (bold added for emphasis).

Moreover, Probate Code Section 21312 states:

"In determining the intent of the transferor, a no contest clause shall be strictly construed."

Strict construction means that it is interpreted against the drafting party whenever consistent with a reasonable interpretation of the settlor's intent.[6]

The Court of Appeals in *Salter v. Lerner* (2009) 176 Cal.App.4th 1184 (under California law which preceded the current, more restrictive, statute governing the enforceability of "no contest" clauses), held that a request for information reasonably necessary to enable beneficiaries to enforce their respective rights does *not* constitute a contest. *Salter* held further that a petition to enforce a trustee's duty is neither a direct nor an indirect challenge to the validity of a trust or its

---

[6] Probate Code Section 21315 provides that: "(a) This part applies to any instrument, whenever executed, that became irrevocable on or after January 1, 2001. …'

terms. *Salter* further held that a pleading to compel an accounting or report of a fiduciary does *not* constitute a contest under California law.

In addition, in California, the Probate Code provides for parties to utilize a procedure in which, in an abundance of caution, the party may ask the Court to predetermine whether a contemplated lawsuit will be deemed to violate a "no contest" provision in a will or trust. This is known as the Safe Harbor procedure and could be utilized if a beneficiary is convinced that negotiations will not resolve a dispute and that litigation against the trustee is imminent.

> **Scenario:** A trust provides for payment by the trustee to the sole beneficiary for her *health, education and welfare* until the beneficiary turns 25 years of age. A so-called **no contest** provision in the trust, however, states as follows:
>
> ### "No Contest Provision
>
> If a person shall in any manner, directly or indirectly, attempt to contest or oppose either the validity, nominations, allocations, divisions or distributions of this Trust, or commences or prosecutes any legal proceedings whatsoever in any jurisdiction to set aside this Agreement or any of its provisions, then in such event such person shall irrevocably and

completely forfeit his or her share, if any, and shall forthwith cease to have any right or interest in the Trust property whatsoever and shall further be deemed to have predeceased the Trustors or the Surviving Trustor."

The trustee fails to account to the 21 year old beneficiary over a period of two years and refuses to pay to her any money whatsoever for tuition, books, food and rent payments to assist her in her on-going post-graduate study in Physiology. The beneficiary files a lawsuit in Court to remove the trustee on the grounds of breach of fiduciary duties—failure to account and failure to administer the trust in good faith, and to have the Court appoint a new trustee in order to, among other things, pay money from the trust for her health, education and welfare. The trustee defends, in part, by claiming that the trust's no contest clause results in a forfeiture of the beneficiary's entire interest in the trust and that therefore she has no standing to sue.

Analysis: A common misperception of a no contest claim is that any claim against the trustee of a trust, and any effort to enforce a good faith administration of the trust will result in the forfeiture created and described in the no contest clause. In this scenario, the language of the no contest clause of the trust does not fit with what the beneficiary is challenging. Here, the beneficiary is not seeking to invalidate the trust or any of its provisions, nor is she seeking to contest the validity of the nominations of the trust, the allocations of assets into the Trust, or any particular distributions intended by the Trust. To the contrary, the beneficiary in her lawsuit is attempting to validate the trust and enforce the Trust by asking the Court to review whether the trustee violated his fiduciary duties and responsibilities created by the trust instrument. The beneficiary is asking that the Court determine whether the trustee has administered the trust in good faith pursuant to the terms of the trust. And the beneficiary is asking for a full and accurate accounting of the disposition of trust property, including perhaps a tracing of assets which have at any time been a part of the trust property, a showing of records in substantiation of any expense claimed in the Administration of the trust for reimbursement to the trustee or otherwise, and a showing that the trustee has managed and invested the trust assets over the years in conformity with the trust instrument provisions. So in conclusion, the beneficiary in this scenario is in a very safe position in regards to application of the no contest provision of the Trust.

CHAPTER 4
A Trustee's Powers

Importantly, a trustee has the powers conferred upon him by the trust itself without any need to obtain court approval. Moreover, unless limited by the terms of the trust, a trustee also has all powers provided to a trustee of a trust as conferred by statute. Probate Code Section 16200.

Unless provided to the contrary in the trust instrument, a trustee has the power to:

(a) acquire or dispose of property, for cash or on credit at public or private sale or exchange. *In re Kessler's Estate* (1953) 120 Cal.App.2d 383 {unless the trust prohibits such a purchase or sale [Probate Code Section 16226; *Giselman v. Starr* (1895) 106 Cal. 651; *Good v. Montgomery* (1898) 119 Cal. 552]}.

(b) borrow or lend money—Probate Code Sections 16241, 16244 and *Purdy*, above;

(c) encumber trust property—Probate Code Section 16228 [unless otherwise proscribed by the trust—*Gardiner v. Cord* (1904) 145 Cal. 157];

(d) enforce claims and defend actions— Probate Code Section 16010;

(e) hire agents to assist the trustee in the management and control of the trust property—Probate Code Section 16247;

(f) pay taxes and expenses—Probate Code Section 16243;

(g) execute and deliver contracts—Probate Code Section 16248;

(h) deposit trust funds at reasonable interest in an insured financial institution account—Probate Code Section 16225(a);

(i) acquire or dispose of property—Probate Code Section 16226;

(j) enter into a lease for any purpose— Probate Code Section 16231; and, enter into an option—Probate Code Section 16233.

The exercise of powers by a trustee, however, is always subject to the trustee's fiduciary duties. Probate Code Section 16202. In the exercise of a trustee's powers, moreover, a trust may afford a trustee with *broad discretion* in the management and control of the trust property. *Estate of Jones* (1977) 68 Cal.

App.3d 274; *Bixby v. Hotchkis* (1943) 58 Cal.App.2d 445. The scope of the allowable discretion is a matter determined by the settlor's intent. *In re Ferrall's Estate* (1953) 41 Cal.3d 166; *In re Caufield's Estate* (1947) 80 Cal.App.2d 443. If a trust expressly gives the trustee broad discretion, a court will not disturb a trustee's decision so long as the trustee has not acted arbitrarily and capriciously toward the affected beneficiary. *Morgan v. Laborers Pension Trust Fund for Northern California* (N.D. Cal. 1977) 433 F.Supp. 518.

The powers and duties of a trustee include doing all acts necessary and expedient to collect, conserve and protect trust assets, to maintain and defend the integrity of the trust for the benefit of the beneficiaries and to employ such assistants as may be necessary for such purposes. *Whittlesey v. Aiello* (2002) 104 Cal.App.4th 1221; *Terry v. Conlan* (2005) 131 Cal. App.4th 1445. A trustee may expend money from the trust for expenses of administration so long as such expenditures are reasonably necessary or appropriate to carry out the purposes of the trust. However, should a trustee exceed its powers and no benefit to the trust estate is bestowed, the trustee will not be entitled to indemnity for such expenditures which will be instead charged to the trustee personally. *Conservatorship of Lefkowitz* (1996) 50 Cal.App.4th 1510. In order for an expense to be chargeable to a trust, the trustee must *subjectively believe* that the expense was necessary or appropriate for the trust's purposes and the trustee must also prove that its belief in that regard was *objectively reasonable. Donahue v. Donahue* (2010) 182 Cal.App.4th 259.

A trial court may, within its sound discretion, conclude that both clerical and professional assistance was necessary in the proper administration of a trust. *In re McLaughlin's Estate* (1954) 43 Cal.2d 462. Attorney's fees reasonably incurred by a trustee in the proper administration of a trust may be properly charged to a trust by the probate court. *David v. Hermann* (2005) 129 CalApp.4th 672; *Hollister v. Hollister* (1961) 194 Cal.App.2d 750. Moreover, it is not only the *right* of a trustee to employ counsel in the administration of a trust, but if necessary in the preservation and execution of the trust, it can be the *legal duty* of a trustee to do so, and in such event counsel is entitled to be paid from the assets of the trust estate. *Bank of America Nat. Trust & Sav. Ass'n v. Long Beach Federal Sav. & Loan Ass'n.* (1956) 141 Cal.App.2d 618. If the trustee is a practicing attorney, however, and chooses to represent himself as trustee in the administration of the trust, such a trustee will not be permitted to charge the trust with attorney's fees. *In re Vokal's Estate,* (1953) 121 Cal.App.2d 252.

However, where an action was brought against the trust as a direct result of a trustee's breach of trust arising from the trustee's greed and indifference, the expenses of defending the trust in such litigation is chargeable not to the trust but to the trustee personally.

In re Baird's Estate (1955) 135 Cal.App.2d 343. Likewise, employment of counsel whose legal services were primarily for a trustee and detrimental to the trust, are not chargeable to the trust. *In re Vokal's Estate, above.*

Scenario: Phillip has been a trustee for the Reynolds Family Trust for the past 15 years, dutifully preparing and filing accountings annually, properly investing and accounting for trust assets, and making periodic distributions in accordance with the terms of the trust. For this work, Phillip has charged the trust, and has been paid, $50.00 per hour of his time as a trustee. This year, however, he decides to transfer the Triangle Ranch property to himself in order to simplify a request for water rights which will benefit not only Triangle Ranch but also the adjacent ranch, Square Road Ranch, owned by the trustee.

The beneficiaries get wind of this transfer and sue Phillip for breach of trust. Phillip employs counsel on behalf of the trust and argues that he acted in good faith and that the trust suffered no damages by virtue of Triangle Ranch being held in his name personally.

Analysis: A trustee owes a duty of full disclosure to the beneficiaries, and a duty of undivided loyalty. Regardless of whether a breach of these duties results in *actual damages* to the trust, the acts depicted in this scenario show a lack of good faith and constitute both a fraud on the trust and a breach of the trustee's fiduciary duties. Phillip would be ordered to transfer the property back to the trust and to pay any damages to the trust caused by his greed and indifference to the interests of the trust. Moreover, the trust would *not* be responsible for payment of fees to the attorney hired by Phillip to act on behalf of the trust since the breach arose as a result of Phillip's greed and indifference to the trust. During the litigation, the beneficiaries would likely be successful in obtaining a temporary restraining order and preliminary injunction *pendente lite* (i.e., during the litigation) restraining the trustee from paying the litigation attorney out of trust funds.

Deviation from the terms of the trust is not justified simply because it would purportedly be "more advantageous" to the beneficiaries or would offer an expedient solution to problems of trust management. *Crocker-Citizens & National Bank v. Younger* (1971) 4 Cal.3d 202. However, a trial court will not permit the "main purpose" of a trust to fail by compelling slavish adherence to administrative limitations of the trust. *Stanton v. Wells Fargo Bank & Union Trust Co.* (1957) 150 Cal.App.2d 763.

Even a grant of absolute subjective discretion in the management and control of a trust may be provided to a trustee by a trust instrument [*Neel v. Barnard* (1944) 24 Cal.2d 406], and such discretion may not be reviewed, directed or overturned by any other person or tribunal. *In re Charters' Estate* (1956) 46 Cal.2d 227. An absolute discretion afforded a trustee by the trust cannot be upset by a court on considerations of the soundness of the exercised discretion. *In re Charters' Estate* (1956) 46 Cal.2d 227. In such a case, the trustee need not act as a reasonable and prudent person under all of the circumstances. *American Center for Education, Inc. v. Cavnar* (1978) 80 Cal.App.3d 476. Where a trustee grants uncontrolled absolute discretion to a trustee, the trustee must simply act in *good faith* consistent with his fiduciary duties. *In re Canfield's Estate* (1947) 80 Cal.App.2d 443. Probate Code Section 16081(a). Instances of bad faith, fraud or abuse of discretion are appropriate issues for court review of the actions of a trustee's "absolute" discretion. *In re Patten's Estate* (1963) 217 Cal. App.2d 167. Where "absolute" discretion is exercised fraudulently, it is subject to review, control and correction by the court. *Penny v. Wilson* (2004) 123 Cal.App.4th 596. Where a trustee exhibits a reckless indifference to the interests of the beneficiaries, a court may properly intervene. *Estate of Collins* (1977) 72 Cal.App.3d 663. The grant of absolute discretion in a trust instrument does not confer upon the trustee immunity from tort liability for breach of his fiduciary duties. *Coberly v. Superior Court for Los Angeles*

Jack's Handy Guide To Trusts

County (1965) 231 Cal.App.2d 685. Moreover, a
trustee's discretion as conferred by a trust, no matter
how broad under the terms of the trust, may *never*
be utilized to obviate the trustor's intentions, nor to
defeat the purpose of the trust. *In re Miller's Estate*
(1964) 259 Cal.App.2d 536.

A trustee may not delegate to another the
performance of duties required to be performed
according to the terms of the trust. Probate Code
Section 16012(a). A trustee may hire professionals
such as real estate agents, accountants and lawyers
to marshal, protect and manage the trust property.
Generally however, ultimately the trustee's duties
regarding the trust are not delegable. *Gaver v. Early*
(1923) 191 Cal. 123; *Estate of Spirtos* (1973) 34 Cal.
App.3d 479. However, investment and management of
specific trust property may be delegated, so long as in
a prudent manner. Probate Code Section 16012(c).

The duty of care by a trustee is simply that a trustee
must exercise at minimum that level of care and
diligence which an ordinarily prudent person would
use in connection with the particular transaction
in the management of his own affairs under the
circumstances. *Bermingham v. Wilcox* (1898) 120 Cal.
467. When it comes to an *expert* trustee, however,
such an expert must use the full extent of his skills and
experience and will be held to a higher standard of
care than a lay person. Probate Code Section 16014;
Werschkull v. United California Bank (1978) 85 Cal.
App.3d 981.

Chapter 4
A Trustee's Powers

Scenario: Bill is appointed as successor trustee, to take control of the trust upon the death of the original Settlor/Trustor/Trustee, Susan. The trust states that the trustee is given "absolute subjective discretion" over the disposition of the trust assets as to when and how to transfer or otherwise make available the trust property to Susan's adult child Elizabeth, except that at the *latest*, the trust property shall be transferred to Elizabeth when Elizabeth reaches the age of 40. Upon Susan's death, Bill places the trust property in a combination of mutual fund, conservative stocks and municipal bonds, renders semi-annual accountings and ignores repeated requests by Elizabeth, now 30, for partial distributions. Also, Bill signs a Power of Attorney over to Susan's probate attorney, Sarah, giving her "full, unlimited and exclusive authority to invest, manage and distribute the trust property in her absolute subjective discretion." Elizabeth files suit for a new trustee based upon breach of the trustee's fiduciary duty and failure to act in good faith.

Analysis: A trustee may hire consultants of various types to assist him or her in managing and administering a trust. Also in some circumstances such as managing investments of trust assets, a trustee may actually delegate such duties to an expert in the field, and rely upon such expert to make sound choices in such investments, subject only to a duty of due care in lay supervision of that expert. However, even with a trust provision conferring absolute subjective discretion to the trustee over trust assets, the trustee still owes a *duty of good faith* in the execution of his duties as a trustee.

When Bill delegated full responsibility to Sarah to make decisions regarding, among other things, distributions to Elizabeth, Bill *violated his duty of good faith*. Even absolute subjective discretion involves the *actual exercise* of discretion and Bill's delegation to Sarah of the responsibility to make decisions precluded Bill from any exercise of discretion. The duty to make a good faith decision as to whether and under what circumstances to make one or more distributions of trust property to a beneficiary is non-delegable. Since Bill repeatedly ignored Sarah's requests for partial distributions, the Court would likely replace Bill with a different trustee who would be instructed by the Court to familiarize himself with

Chapter 4
A Trustee's Powers

the trust, the trust property and the beneficiary's circumstances and make a decision whether and in what manner to make one or more distributions to Sarah prior to Sarah's 40th birthday.

CHAPTER 5
Information Flow

"Knowledge is power. Information is power.
The secreting or hoarding of knowledge
or information may be an act of tyranny
camouflaged as humility."

Robin Morgan

trustee must reasonably inform the beneficiaries of both the trust and its administration. Probate Code Section 16060. Generally, on request by a beneficiary, a trustee must report to the beneficiary on the requested information as pertains to the trust property subject to the beneficiary's interest. Probate Code Section 16061. A beneficiary has a right to inspect the trustee's records pertaining to the trust property. *Strauss v. Superior Court In and For Los Angeles County* (1950) 36 Cal.2d 396. Accordingly, a trustee has a duty to prepare, retain and maintain full and accurate accounts of the trustee's transactions regarding the trust. *Purdy v. Johnson* (1917) 174 Cal. 521. In *Purdy*, the California Supreme Court *reversed* a trial court ruling which had in effect placed the burden upon the beneficiary *to disprove* conclusionary statements in a long-overdue accounting. The trial court had invited the beneficiary to simply cross-examine the accounting expert who prepared the accounting from incomplete records. *Purdy* held that the trial court's procedure had the burden of proof backwards and held instead that it is incumbent upon the trustee to *affirmatively account* for all trust property and its disposition and to provide adequate back-up substantiation of such accounts.

On demand (in accordance with the timing allowed for by the trust or by statute), and so long as the trust may not still be *revoked* [Probate Code Section 16069(a)], a trustee *must* render an accounting of all such transactions. *Purdy, above.* This entitlement to an accounting includes a right to an accounting as to rents and profits from trust property. *Keogh v. Noble* (1902) 136 Cal. 153.

California statute requires that a trustee account to all beneficiaries *at least annually,* at the trust's termination and at any change of trustees. Probate Code Section 16062(a). Regarding personal liability of a trustee, in the event a trustee refuses or negligently neglects to keep true accounts, *all presumptions* otherwise created by the trust or statute *are against him. Blackmon v. Hale* (1970) 1 Cal.3d 548; *Purdy, above; Bone v. Hayes* (1908) 154 Cal. 759. A court, moreover, in the sound exercise of its broad equitable powers, may compel an accounting by a trustee. *Evangelho v. Presoto* (1998) 67 Cal.App.4th 615.

Jack's Handy Guide To Trusts

If visitation of and talking with a child is necessary for the proper administration of a trust, and the child's parents or guardians do not cooperate, a trustee may obtain a court order fixing the time, place and circumstances for such visits. *In re Kessler's Estate* (1953) 120 Cal.App.2d 383.

> **Scenario:** A successor trustee, Wanda, has various trust property assets under her control, including cash, a savings account, parcels of real property, and indebtedness owed to the trust by various third parties. Wanda has been the trustee of the trust for the past eight years, has received compensation from the trust for her trustee services, and has never created or produced an accounting of any kind as to the trust property and its disposition. The beneficiary, Samantha, is supported by regular payments from the trust and is entitled pursuant to the express terms of the trust to take over control of all of the remaining trust property upon turning 25. At age 19, Samantha demands an accounting. Instead, Wanda turns over to Samantha a banker's box of receipts, checking account statements and deeds. The four-year statute of limitations on collection of a Note in default for $50,000.00 owed to the trust has expired. Samantha sues Wanda for breach of

fiduciary duty and resulting losses of trust property and income to the trust property, and seeks an accounting and a change in trustees to be ordered by the Court.

Analysis: Wanda apparently treated her responsibilities as trustee of the trust as if it were a matter of her own personal business which she decided to neglect. Unfortunately for Wanda (and for Samantha if Wanda has no assets to go after in enforcement of any Judgment against Wanda), once the position of trustee is accepted or otherwise acted upon by a proposed trustee, *fiduciary duties arise and personal liability attaches* for failing to comply with those fiduciary duties. In this case, Wanda failed to make at least annual accountings to Samantha, and this alone is a violation of Wanda's fiduciary duty to account. Without accountings, or other access to records, Samantha would have no way of knowing whether and to what extent Wanda was safeguarding the assets of the trust and was generating proper income for the trust through sound investment strategies. During most of the time period in question, Samantha was a minor, but in California, a beneficiary has three years[7] from the date

---

[7] Probate Code Section 16460(a)(1).

an accounting is delivered within which to contest a claim which is first adequately disclosed in the accounting[8]. In this case, however, no accounting whatsoever was prepared. Instead, a mass of disorganized documents were turned over to Samantha who was left to analyze them herself. In court, Samantha would simply need to prove what trust property existed at the outset of the trust, and from this point on, Wanda, as trustee, would have the burden of proving that those trust assets had been preserved, that adequate income had been generated from those trust assets and that any transmutations of trust property (for example, selling a parcel of real property for cash plus a secured Note) had preserved the value of the trust property for later enforcement. The court would likely order Wanda to prepare proper accountings. It would be *Wanda's burden* to trace the trust assets and its income, and to the extent that she could not do so with adequate documentary or other substantiation, Wanda would be

---

[8] As to a minor, this period of three years commences when the accounting is received by the minor's guardian, or, if the minor does not have a guardian, when it is received by the minor's parent so long as the parent does not have a conflict of interest. Probate Code Section 16460(b)(3).

held *personally liable* for the loss to the trust. Regarding enforcement of the Note where the statute of limitation for enforcement was passed, if the debtor raises this defense and otherwise fails to pay off the Note, Wanda would be personally liable for the value of the unpaid principal plus interest of that Note. The Court would also order that Wanda be replaced as trustee by a person or entity who/which would properly discharge the fiduciary duties of trustee.

CHAPTER 6
Undivided Loyalty

As long as the trustor of a revocable *inter vivos* trust is *still alive and competent,* the trustee owes a duty solely to the trustor and *not* to the beneficiaries. *In re Estate of Giraldin* (2012) 55 Cal.4th 1058. That duty of loyalty shifts to the beneficiaries once all trustors of the trust are no longer competent or are deceased.

Although a trustee has a duty of complete loyalty to the beneficiaries to the exclusion of all other parties [*N.L.R.B. v. Amax Coal Co. etc.* (1981) 453 U.S. 322], a trustee must always give first and primary deference to the best interests of the trust itself. *Toedter v. Bradshww* (1958) 164 Cal.App.2d 200. A trustee must act honestly, in good faith and within the limits of his discretion as a trustee of the particular trust instrument. *American Center for Education, Inc. v. Cavnar* (1978) 80 Cal.App.3d 476. A trustee must exercise *independent judgment* and may not comply automatically with demands of a beneficiary. *Morse v. Crocker National Bank* (1983) 142 Cal.App.3d 228.

A trustee may not participate in any transaction with the trust in which the trustee has an interest adverse to the trust's beneficiaries, and may not use trust property for his own profit or for any purpose unconnected with the trust. Probate Code Section 16004(a); *Lix v. Edwards* (1978) 82 Cal.App.3d 573, 581. Thus, any secret trustee profits would constitute a violation of a trustee's fiduciary duty and duty to disclose all material facts. *Uzyel v. Kadisha* (2010) 188 Cal.App.4th 866. The origin of the rule proscribing the holding of adverse interests by a trustee is older than statutory law. *Sims v. Petaluma Gas Light Co.* (1901) 131 Cal. 656 [63 P. 1011]; *Broder v. Conklin* (1898) 121 Cal. 282.

If a trustee uses trust property or his powers in such a manner as to personally profit to the detriment of the beneficiaries, all profit or other advantage so received by him is deemed to be held in *constructive trust* for and belong to the beneficiaries. *Purdy, above.*

As a matter of criminal law in California, a trustee who misappropriates trust property to any use or purpose not within the scope of the trust, or who secrets such trust property with a fraudulent intent to misdirect the use of such property, may be charged and convicted, upon competent proof, of the crime of embezzlement. California Penal Code Section 506.

> **Scenario:** A trustee, Sam, is given control over trust property including a 15-carat "flawless" diamond. The description of the diamond in the trust instrument is vague and Sam decides to substitute

his wife's 1.5 carat diamond for the trust diamond. He places the trust diamond in a safe deposit box opened under an alias. Sam also leases to himself and his wife, for a one-year period, a residential rental property, owned by the trust, at roughly 60% of the going market rate. The beneficiary of the trust, Jill, hears of the lease transaction and the lease rate, and thereafter gives Sam a request to examine all of the trust property and accounts. During the ensuing examination process, Jill believes she recognizes that the diamond shown by Sam to her is actually *Sam's wife's wedding ring diamond.* Jill files suit against Sam for breach of fiduciary duty and lodges a police report with the local police, alleging embezzlement of the trust diamond.

Analysis: As is often the case, a breach by a trustee of the duty of loyalty can also signal the occurrence of other nefarious behavior. Crimes of embezzlement are easily proved, once suspected, since it is typically a matter of simply tracing the asset. In this instance, Sam violated his duty of loyalty by self-dealing himself and his wife into a lease at a substantial 40% reduction in the fair market value lease rate. This transaction, in turn, caused Jill to

Chapter 6
Undivided Loyalty

want to look more carefully at the rest of the trust property and accounts.

For the breach of the duty of loyalty, the Court could discharge Sam as trustee, substitute a new trustee, break the lease with Sam and order Sam to pay damages to the trust for the rental income lost while Sam and his wife held the leasehold interest at the 40% reduction in monthly lease rate.

As to the trust diamond, Jill could prove that Sam's wife could no longer produce her wedding diamond, and from personal knowledge within the family, that the trust diamond was highly valuable. Diamonds of this size and quality are typically appraised and insured, and this diamond was no exception. An examination of the trust checking account revealed payment of the insurance premium on the diamond, which led Jill to the insurer itself, which in turn led to photos and a full appraisal of this remarkable stone.

Sam used cash and a false identity to open an account and rent a safety deposit box in which to conceal the trust diamond, but Sam revealed the location of the trust diamond to police once they interrogated him regarding the incident. Although

Jack's Handy Guide To Trusts

Sam claimed he had placed the trust diamond in the safe deposit box in order to *safeguard* it, this would likely be rejected by a Judge or Jury in a criminal prosecution for embezzlement. The trier of fact would consider that Sam had substituted his wife's wedding diamond for the trust diamond in the showing of trust property to Jill and had rented the safe deposit box under an alias with a falsified identification card. Sam would probably serve in the neighborhood of 6 months in County Jail as a condition of his felony probation for grand theft embezzlement.

A trustee must keep and maintain trust property segregated from all other property not a part of the trust, and must maintain a designation for such property as belonging to the trust. Probate Code Section 16009. This of course includes an obligation to keep a beneficiary's money separate, free from liabilities which a trustee may have in the use of his own funds. In this regard a trustee may not commingle his own funds with a beneficiary's funds without express authorization from the beneficiary. *In re Armstrong* (1886) 69 Cal. 239. Failure to keep trust assets separate from the trustee's personal assets results in the trustee incurring *absolute liability* for their safety and for the value of their use. *In re Bane* (1898) 120 Cal. 533, 536; *Estate of McLellan* (1936) 8 Cal.2d 49, 54.

Chapter 6
Undivided Loyalty

Scenario: A trustee deposits trust money in a bank in his own name without designation of the trust and without indication of the trustee's representative character. The trust funds are executed upon by the trustee's personal creditors.

Analysis: The trustee is personally liable to the trust for the loss. *In re Woods Estate and Guardianship* (1911) 120 Cal. 533; *In re Arguello's Estate* (1892) 97 Cal. 196. Moreover, the trustee has committed a breach of fiduciary duty by depositing the funds into his own bank account and could be removed and replaced as trustee by a court of competent legal jurisdiction.

A trustee must not in effect *negotiate with himself* in striking any deal with the trust, and in the event that he does so, the transaction will be held as invalid, subject to being set aside at the option of the beneficiary, *regardless of the fairness of the transaction. Wickersham v. Crittenden* (1892) 93 Cal. 17; *Howard's Estate* (1955) 133 Cal.App.2d 535; *Smith v. Pacific Vinegar & Pickle Works* (1904) 145 Cal. 352; *Toedter v. Bradshaw* (1958) 164 Cal.App.2d 200; *Differding v. Ballagh* (1932) 121 Cal.App. 1. Self-dealing is an obvious violation of a trustee's fiduciary duty to the beneficiary. For example, where a trustee has the power to sell certain trust property and sells it to himself, a breach of trust results regardless of the trustee's good faith or the lack of injury to the beneficiary. *Differding v. Ballagh* (1932) 121 Cal.App. 1, 6, 8.

> "This rule is based on sound public policy, and there also enters into it the legal principle that, in order to make an express contract, there must be the assent of two separate independent minds; that no man can effectually make a contract with himself." *Smith, above,* 145 Cal. at 362.

Where *multiple trustees* are *jointly* responsible for administration of all of the trust assets, they may not simply agree with impunity to divide control of various trust assets. In such a case, each trustee will be responsible not only for their own actions regarding the trust, but also for the actions of the other trustees. *Birmingham v. Wilcox* (1898) 120 Cal. 467.

> **Scenario:** Two joint trustees are appointed as trustees for a trust containing funds and real estate. The trustees decided between themselves, and without authority of the trust, to divide responsibility for managing the trust assets. Trustee #1 managed the commercial real estate and leased out the properties at market rates and terms, and secured payment to the trust. Trustee #2 used a portion of the trust funds to

purchase bonds for himself. The bonds lose all value and Trustee #2 is without assets to repay the trust. The beneficiaries file suit against Trustee #1 for breach of fiduciary duty and loss of income.

Analysis: The beneficiary need not sue all trustees where one has no assets. The court would hold Trustee #1 liable to the trust for the acts of Trustee #2 who used trust property for himself and not for trust purposes. Trustee #1's purported delegation of responsibility to Trustee #2 would *not* absolve the former of personal liability.

But dealing with trust assets in good faith is not in itself enough to discharge the duties of a trustee. In the case of *Purdy*, discussed *above*, a trial court expressly found that the trustees had dealt with trust property properly, in "good faith" and without any intention to deceive or overreach, and it exonerated the trustees from liability to the beneficiary for losses and gaps in trust accounting information. On appeal, the California Supreme Court *reversed* the trial court's judgment, holding,

> "But conceding the good faith of the trustees, the fact remains that they had, by their own admission, failed to comply with the obligation which rests upon all trustees to keep full and accurate accounts of the trust funds coming into their hands, and to

render a full account of all of their dealings with the trust fund [citation], and where there has been a negligent failure to keep true accounts, or a refusal to account, all presumptions will be against the trustee upon a settlement [citations]." *Purdy, above,* at 527.

Thus, the trial court in *Purdy* erred in holding that the burden of proof was on the beneficiary to point out where the accounting was erroneous. The trial court had permitted an expert to create an accounting for the trial and then required the beneficiary to cross-examine the expert about the particulars, with no testimony of the expert on direct examination. *Purdy* pointed out that this procedure was the *opposite* of what should have occurred,

> "The entire trial was conducted upon the erroneous theory that the burden of proof was upon the beneficiary to point out the particulars in which the accounting was erroneous, and that she was bound to go forward and establish affirmatively the impropriety of the charges and credits which she assailed. Such is not the law.... Even if we accept the ultimate finding [of the trial court] as technically sufficient, it must be held the trustees failed to prove an accounting that would justify the judgment under review." *Purdy, above,* at 527-528.

CHAPTER 7
Advantage: Beneficiary

It is presumed to be a violation of a trustee's fiduciary duty to a beneficiary of a trust if, during the existence of the confidential relationship, an advantage is gained by the trustee from the beneficiary of the trust. If a trustee's position is improved through a transaction between the trustee and the beneficiary of the trust, such as in the case of gaining a favorable opportunity, benefit or profit, an advantage has been obtained. *Rader v. Thrasher* (1962) 57 Cal.2d 244 (during the existence of an attorney-client relationship, the attorney entered into a contingency fee agreement with the client); and, *Lail v. Lail* (1955) 133 Cal.App.2d 610. In *Agam v. Gavra* (Cal.App. 6th Dist. 2015) WL 1843009, the court held that a contract entered into between a trustee and the trust's beneficiary by which the trustee gains an advantage is voidable by the beneficiary. The advantage, in order to result in a breach of fiduciary duty, does not need to be an unfair, unjust or inequitable advantage. The presumption is that the trustee gets the superior bargain in *every* transaction with a beneficiary of the trust. *Rader, above; Ball v.*

Jack's Handy Guide To Trusts

Posey (1986) 176 Cal.App.3d 1209; *Lail, above*; *Stiles v. Cain* (1901) 134 Cal. 170.

> "The rule is older than the Code, and is, that such a contract [between a trustee and his beneficiary], [even] without any proof of unfairness, is voidable at the option of the beneficiary, but 'it is possible for the trustee to overcome the presumption of invalidity.' (2 Pomeroy's Equity Jurisprudence, Sec. 958.) The rule which was codified declared the presumption to be, that the trustee got the best in every transaction with his beneficiary, and did not give an adequate consideration for what he got. To say that the beneficiary must prove that the consideration was inadequate, is to reverse this time-honored rule." *Stiles, above*, at 172-173.

In any transaction between a trustee and a beneficiary under a trust, during either the existence of the trust or, as a question of fact, while the influence of the trustee over the beneficiary remains, a statutory rebuttable presumption arises that such transaction constitutes a violation of the trustee's fiduciary duties. Probate Code Section 16004(c). *Tognazzini v. Tognazzina* (1954) 125 Cal.App.2d 679. The presumption of violation of fiduciary duties in this situation may be rebutted by the trustee upon

Chapter 7
Advantage: Beneficiary

proof that there was fair disclosure, there was no overreaching and the beneficiary affected acted voluntarily and with full understanding. *Rader v. Thrasher* (1962) 57 Cal.2d 244; *Buchmayer v. Buchmayer* (1945) 68 Cal.App.2d 462; *Kisling v. Shaw* (1867) 33 Cal. 425 (arm's length transaction). The sole and uncorroborated testimony of the trustee, however, is not legally adequate to rebut the presumption. *In re Raphael's Estate* (1953) 115 Cal. App.2d 525. This rule is a corollary to the rule that where a fiduciary gains an advantage in dealing with a principal, a presumption of undue influence arises. *Ball v. Posey* (1986) 176 Cal.App.3d 1209. Moreover, it is not incumbent upon a beneficiary to prove an inadequacy of consideration or that the deal between him and the trustee was an unfair one, because to require this of a beneficiary would reverse the presumption. *Bradmer v. Vasquez* (1986) 176 Cal. App.3d 1209; *Stiles v. Cain* (1901) 134 Cal. 170.

> **Scenario:** A trust establishes that Blackwater, a residential 4-plex, be held in trust for the benefit of John until John turns 30 years of age, and then transferred to John. Prior to the transfer, John is to receive all net rents after trust administrative expenses. Trustee enters a lease with John for 3 years with John as a tenant in one of the units at a monthly rate, and a second lease with himself in another similar unit at the same monthly

rate. After six months, John moves out, declares both leases to be invalid and demands that the trustee also moves out, cancels both leases and pays damages to the trust for a deficiency between the monthly rate and the fair market value of the units.

Analysis: In this instance, the trustee has placed himself in a very compromising situation since he in effect based his own, personal, residential lease agreement upon the terms of the residential lease agreement entered into with the beneficiary. An inference might be that John's lease rate is at least fair market value or less, as an indirect benefit to John; but if the lease rate is *below* fair market value as to John, then it is *also* favoring the trustee in the trustee's personal residential lease. On the other hand, if the lease rate is *above* the fair market value, and since the trustee has negotiated directly with the beneficiary in setting the lease rate, the lease is clearly voidable at the election of the beneficiary, John. Although the trustee would have the opportunity to try to overcome the presumption of invalidity, in this case the trustee would be unlikely to prevail, since he personally received

Chapter 7
Advantage: Beneficiary

the benefit of the same lease rate as afforded John, the trust beneficiary. Upon proof that the lease rates were below fair market value, the trustee would be liable to the trust for the loss of income to the trust on both leases.

CHAPTER 8
Taking Control

After reading and understanding the trust instrument itself, the next likely act by a trustee in the proper discharge of his duty to the trust would be to take and keep control of, and to preserve, the trust property. Probate Code Section 16006. This duty is a continuing one and lasts until, in accordance with the trust and in the permitted sound discretion of the trustee, disposition of that property should be made. For a testamentary trustee (a trustee of a trust which springs into existence upon someone's death) the trustee must take reasonable steps to require the executors of the decedent's estate to transfer to the trust any property as to which they have a duty to transfer. *In re Prior's Estate* (1952) 111 Cal.App.2d 464.

A trustee must do all acts necessary and expedient to maintain the trust for the benefit of the beneficiaries and to employ such persons as required to accomplish such purposes. *Terry v. Conlan* (2005) 131 Cal.App.4th 1445; *Whittlesey v. Aiello* (2002) 104 Cal.App.4th 1221. This includes the authority to commence and prosecute litigation necessary to recover trust property. *In re Bouche's Estate* (1937) 24 Cal.App.2d 86.

Chapter 8
Taking Control

In protecting and preserving assets of the trust, a trustee has a duty to protect that trust against unnecessary liability, expenses and claims. *In re Rawitzer's Estate* (1917) 174 Cal. 585. In these regards, a trustee must use reasonable care to make the trust property productive, in the sense of earning adequate income. Probate Code Sections 16227 and 16229.

> **Scenario:** A trustee fails to fence an unimproved property and fails to mark it with a sign, as allowed by statute, regarding adverse use. Neighbors walk diagonally across the property for over 5 years in order to cross between the 7-Eleven store and their home. After five years, trustee lists the property for sale and the Neighbors file an action to establish a prescriptive easement for continuous, adverse, hostile use of the walking path.

> **Analysis:** Since it is the duty of a trustee to preserve and protect trust property, and since a trustee has a right to bring an action (litigation) to prevent waste or trespass on the trust property, the trustee would be personally liable for any loss of value to the property by virtue of the prescriptive easement lawfully acquired over time for the Neighbors to walk their path to the 7-Eleven. The trustee could have fenced the property or posted the

statutory notice or filed suit to halt the continuing trespass. Having failed to do so, the trustee became personally liable for the loss in value to the trust, or the cost in buying back the prescriptive easement, whichever is less. *See, Younglove v. Hacker* (1936) 15 Cal.App.2d 211.

A trust intended to manage certain property carries an implication that the trustee is to *retain such property under his or her control* and such implication is inconsistent with any action by the trustee to sell or otherwise dispose of the property. *Goad, above.* In *Wood v. American National Bank* (1932) 125 Cal.App. 248, the court held that where a trust provision provided that the beneficiaries may occupy certain trust property as a home, the trust necessarily implied that the trustee has no power to sell that residential property.

Occasionally, the trustee may have not only the power to sell an asset, but the legal duty. For example, if the trust requires the settlor to subsidize any deficits in net income and directs the trustee to sell trust property to augment such net income to the extent the settlor is in default, the trustee is under an obligation to sell the property if reasonably necessary to comply with the terms of the trust. *Allen v. Blair* (1936) 13 Cal. App.2d 227.

And where the trust directs the trustee to sell trust property and to divide the proceeds, it is implied that the trustee must make reasonable efforts to sell within a reasonable period of time [*Campbell v. Kennedy* (1918) 177 Cal. 430], but not so quickly as to result in a sale below the reasonable market value in a sacrifice sale. *In re Heberle's Estate* (1909) 155 Cal. 723.

The terms of a trust must be followed in the sale of trust property. So, for example, if the trust provides that a particular sale must be approved in advance by a beneficiary, such approval is considered to be a *condition precedent* to the lawful transfer, and a trustee's deed without such approval would be inoperative to convey title. *Sprague v. Edwards* (1874) 48 Cal. 239. Joint execution and acknowledgement of the trustee's deed adequately proves such approval. *Welton v. Palmer* (1870) 39 Cal. 456.

Should the trust prohibit the sale of certain property, however, *any* purported conveyance is in excess of the trustee's powers. *Dougherty v. California Kettleman Oil Royalties* (1939) 13 Cal.2d 174 (transfer of trust property by trustee in violation of rights of beneficiary constitutes a fraud on the beneficiary).

Unless prohibited in the trust, a trustee has the power to enter into a lease for a term within or beyond the term of the trust. *Church v. Church* (1940) 40 Cal.App.2d 696. The power of a trustee to enter into such a lease, however, may be expressly or impliedly prohibited by the trust. *Drinkhouse v. Birch Ranch & Oil Co.* (1950) 97 Cal.App.2d 923 (trust was created in order to promptly liquidate a business and sell its assets; no power of trustee to make an oil and gas lease for years could be implied).

A trustee may, unless contrary to the provisions of the trust, vote and give proxies as to shares of a domestic or foreign corporate or other entity, and waive notice and approve actions taken by such entity or its shareholders, members or owners. Probate Code Section 16234.

> **Scenario:** A trustee states that a beneficiary shall be provided with adequate support until the beneficiary turns 30 years of age, at which time the remaining trust assets shall be transferred to the beneficiary. Income from stock and rental property is adequate to meet this purpose for a period of time, but then the value of the stock sharply declines. Thereafter, the trustee promptly and substantially reduces payments to levels inadequate to support the beneficiary, explaining that the trust property income is insufficient and that the trustee must maintain the trust property for later distribution to the beneficiary when he turns 30. The beneficiary files suit for breach of fiduciary duty regarding preservation of the trust assets, for an accounting, and to compel the trustee to

pay to the beneficiary adequate support, until the beneficiary turns 30.

Analysis: A trustee not only has the power to sell trust property, it has *a duty* to sell in the event that the trust creates an obligation to support a beneficiary. In this case, the stock value declined and it is unclear in the example whether the cause was a lack of reasonable diligence in administering the stock portfolio, or whether the stock market simply took an unexpected turn for the worse, beyond the reasonable control of the trustee. Discovery and expert opinion would decide that issue in the litigation, and if a fiduciary breach occurred, the trustee would be held personally liable for the loss. If the support obligation of the trust cannot in any event reasonably be accomplished without depleting trust assets by sale, then a trustee is under a duty to sell a portion or all of such assets in order to meet the trust's obligation of adequate support of the beneficiary. *Allen v. Blair* (1936) 13 Cal.App.2d 227.

But what happens if a good faith lawsuit by a beneficiary is unsuccessful and the trust's attorney's fees are in excess of all of the liquid assets of the trust?

Jack's Handy Guide To Trusts

Scenario: A trustee hires an attorney to defend the trust against a breach of trust lawsuit by one of the beneficiaries, who claims that the trustee treated him less favorably than his sister. Although the trustee prevails in the protracted and acrimonious lawsuit, the attorney fees incurred by the trust are in excess of all of the liquid assets of the trust. The trustee conveys a parcel of improved real property to the attorney in full satisfaction of the attorney's fees and costs. Once the male beneficiary hears of this transfer, he threatens suit again.

Analysis: While a trustee may not gift trust property to anyone, where a trust allows for real property to be transferred for trust purposes, a trustee may convey land to an agent as compensation for services in the furtherance of the trust. *Mansfield v. District Agr. Ass'n No. 6* (1908) 154 Cal. 145. When the trust's counsel sends a letter to the aggrieved beneficiary explaining his attorney's fees and costs and citing the *Mansfield* case for the propriety of the land transfer, the beneficiary would likely back off of his litigious threats.

Chapter 8
Taking Control

Even the advice of a trustee's own lawyer cannot shield the trustee from liability due to a loss. *Martin, above.* The rule applies regardless of whether the person to whom the care of the trust property is entrusted by the trustee, is a stranger, an attorney or even a co-trustee. *Gaver, above; Bermingham, above.*

As a corollary to the duty of a trustee to protect and preserve trust property, a trustee has a duty to defend trust assets against adverse claims. Probate Code Section 16011. Any unjustified failure to defend against adverse claims against trust property subjects a trustee to personal liability. *Metzenbaum v. Metzenbaum* (1953) 115 Cal.App.2d 395. Such a power and duty, of course, includes the authority to pay and settle any claim and to release any claim held by the trust. Probate Code Section 16242.

> **Scenario:** Trustee holds trust funds in a bank account designated as a trust account. Trustee's creditor levies against the trust account and Bank pays over all of the trust funds in partial satisfaction of the levy. The trust funds would have been exempt from levy had a claim of exemption been properly pursued. However, no notification to the trustee or to the beneficiary was given by Bank.
>
> **Analysis:** The trustee cannot avoid personal liability by relinquishing control over trust property to a third party bank.

However, the trustee could sue the Bank for breach of fiduciary duty and for indemnification against liability to the beneficiaries for failing to notify the beneficiaries and trustee such that proper claims of exemption could be pursued. *Charles Hing v. Joe Lee* (1918) 37 Cal. App.313.

Another way of describing the duty to make trust assets work and earn income is to say that a trustee must make trust property *productive* in the reasonable furtherance of the interests of the trust. Probate Code Section 16227.

Scenario: Trustee sells a trust property house, receives testamentary distributions from the trustor's estate and places all of the approximately $400,000.00 into a checking account bearing no interest for three years. At the end of three years, the beneficiaries ask for an accounting and the trustee immediately invests all but $35,000.00 of such funds to purchase for the trust an interest-bearing money market account.

Analysis: While an amount of cash reasonably adequate for month-to-month administration of a trust may be retained in a non-interest-bearing account, the

remainder of the cash assets must be
reasonably invested at secure market rates
to render the trust property productive.
Trustee would be liable to the trust for the
loss of income from a reasonably prudent
investment of approximately $365,000.00
for the period of three years when the
cash was retained in the checking account
with no interest.

Unless prohibited by the trust itself, or by Order of
the court, a trustee has the power to organize and run
a business that constitutes trust property. Probate Code
Section 16222(a). If the trust requires that all assets of
the business be liquidated at a certain point in time,
the business may be operated for a reasonable period
of time pending such sale or liquidation, or pending a
court hearing. Probate Code Section 16222(c).

When reasonably necessary in the proper discharge
of a trustee's duties under the trust, a trustee may
hire and compensate experts, including attorneys,
accountants, auditors, appraisers, investment advisors
and other persons. Probate Code Section 16247.
Where employment of such a person is reasonably
necessary to enable a trustee to perform his duties
in the trust, the trustee may be held personally liable
for any failure to employ and follow the advice of
such a person. *Bank of America...etc v. Long Beach
Federal Sav. & Loan Ass'n* (1956) 141 Cal.App.2d 618.
Notwithstanding a trustee's power to hire persons to

assist him in the execution of his duties as trustee of a trust, a trustee *may not delegate duties which he ought to personally perform.* Probate Code Section 16012(a). A trustee's duty to manage and administer a trust is *personal* and generally not delegable. *Gaver,* above; *Estate of Spirtos* (1973) 34 Cal.App.3d 479.

However, where a trustee has properly delegated a matter to a person, the trustee has only a duty to exercise *general supervision* over the person. Probate Code Section 16012(b), (c) and Section 16052. The delegation by a trustee of "investment and management functions" have special rules set forth in Probate Code Sections 16012(c) and 16052. As to investment and management functions, a trustee may delegate "as prudent under the circumstances." Prudence requires the exercise of reasonable care in:

1. selecting an agent;

2. establishing the scope and terms of the delegation, consistent with the purposes and terms of the trust; and,

3. periodically reviewing the agent's overall performance and compliance with the terms of the delegation. Probate Code Section 16052(a), (b)

A trustee is not liable to the trust as to delegation of investment and management functions so long as he complies with the foregoing. Probate Code Section 16052(c).

Scenario: Trust property includes the $400,000.00 proceeds of a life insurance policy. Trustee receives and deposits the $400,000.00 into a trust checking account. Trustee then hires and delegates investment and management authority to a reputable investment Advisor, complete with a commitment by the Advisor to regularly monitor the investment and to make any adjustments reasonably necessary from time to time to keep the investment funds productive. The Advisor purchases, on behalf of the trust, $350,000.00 of value in a reputable money market account, pays himself a fee and never again reviews the money market account holding. Trustee thereafter fails to make periodic accountings. Three years later, the trustee checks the money market account records for the first time since the original purchase and determines that the money market account lost a steady average of 15% per year, where average returns of money market accounts were a positive 5% per annum over the same period of time. Trustee provides an accounting to the beneficiaries covering the entire three year period. The Advisor went out of business two years ago and moved to Kazakhstan to follow his dream of weaving rugs.

Jack's Handy Guide To Trusts

Analysis: The failure to regularly account shifts the burden to trustee to prove each and every transaction as being in accord with the terms and conditions of the trust. (*Purdy, above*). However, in this case, trustee properly describes the allocation of the trust funds and claims he properly delegated the investment and management duties to the reputable money market fund Advisor.

Although potentially the trustee could have sued the Advisor for breach of fiduciary duty and indemnity, he will be hard pressed to collect when the Advisor now lives in Kazakhstan and is weaving rugs for a living. Instead, trustee has positioned himself as the *exclusive target* of a lawsuit by the beneficiaries for breach of fiduciary duty and loss of income by the failure to make the money market funds productive. Although authority for the money market fund purchase was initially proper, trustee failed to *periodically review* the Advisor's overall performance and compliance with the terms of the delegation. Consequently, when the trust funds tied up in the failing money market fund should have been moved to a more productive money market fund, they were not moved.

The Advisor never checked up on the investment and annual yield, and trustee failed to check up on the Advisor. Trustee would be held personally liable for breach of fiduciary duty and liable to the trust for losses and lost income for at least 2, and probably 2½ to 2¾ years. An expert might testify that a steady decline of 15% per annum when other money market funds are averaging positive annual yields of 5% should not be permitted longer than one or at most two quarters.

As to the $50,000.00 retained in the checking account, a trustee may hold "an amount of trust property reasonably necessary for the orderly administration of the trust in the form of cash or in a checking account without interest." Probate Code Section 16225(e)

Regardless of any power to delegate powers, however,

"if a trustee enters into any arrangement in relation to trust funds which surrenders or limits his control over them, he becomes a guarantor of the fund, irrespective of his motive, or whether his surrender of control was the cause of the loss of the fund." *Gaver, above.*

See also, Martin v. Bank of America (1935) 4 Cal. App.2d 431. In *Gaver,* the trustee abdicated control over trust funds to her attorney, who fraudulently concealed and omitted the funds from all accounts and misappropriated a large part for his own use (at 125). *Gaver* held that the attorney became the agent for the trustee, "to whom she attempted to delegate her duties as trustee. She had no right to shift her duty to him." (at 127). The court wrote further,

> "If a trustee confides the application of a trust fund to the care of another, whether a stranger or his own attorney or solicitor, or even a co-trustee, he will be held personally responsible for any loss that may result. Under such circumstances a trustee may employ attorneys or agents, according to the usual course of business, to reduce the estate to possession and protect it, but when once in his hands his personal duty to dispose and manage it begins, and this duty is not to be delegated. [citations]." (at 127)

In *Gaver,* the California Supreme Court held that the negligent delegation to the attorney of her duties as trustee, her abandonment to the attorney of the management and control of the trust property and her failure, "to examine and make any inquiry concerning the correctness of the several accounts prepared by Early, filed by her as such guardian, and presented to the court," requires imposition against the trustee of damages with interest at the legal rate compounded annually and not merely with "simple" (i.e., *not* compounded annually) interest. (at 127-128). Thus, as shown in *Gaver,* even delegation to an attorney who holds a fiduciary duty to the trust will not absolve a trustee from his personal duties under the trust and will not shield a trustee from personal liability to the full extent of the fiduciary's misdeeds and omissions.

CHAPTER 9
Making Assets Work

Fundamental in a trustee's duties is the duty to invest trust property so as to make it work and earn income. Probate Code Section 16007; *Allen v. Hussey* (1950) 101 Cal.App.2d 457; *Bemmerly v. Woodward* (1899) 124 Cal. 568. A trustee's neglect to use reasonable care to make trust property productive is a breach of the trustee's fiduciary duty. *Gaver v. Early* (1923) 191 Cal. 123, 125; *Lynch v. John M. Redfield Foundation* (1970) 9 Cal.App.3d 293, 298.

This duty does not require a trustee to invest funds too small to be prudently invested, but if there is an unreasonable delay in investing more substantial sums, the trustee is in breach of his fiduciary duties and incurs personal liability for the loss of income. *Van de Kamp v. Bank of America* (1988) 204 Cal.App.3d 819; *Uzyel v. Kadisha* (2010) 188 Cal.App.4th 866; *Lynch v. John M. Redfield Foundation* (1970) 9 Cal.App.3d 293; Probate Code Sections 16440 and 16441. An absence of a trustee's personal motive to personally gain an advantage from the failure to invest is *irrelevant.* Probate Code Sections 16440 and 16441.

Chapter 9
Making Assets Work

Scenario: A trust requires that a 10% interest-per-annum note in the principal sum of $240,000.00 be paid off at maturity on January 1, 2020 (approximately three years away). The trust established a cash deposit for this purpose, of which $340,000.00 remains. The trust has a total of $400,000.00 cash in a bank account bearing simple interest at .15 percent per annum (i.e., less than 1% per year). The cash deposit pays the interest on the note. The beneficiary complains that the deposit account bears insufficient interest and that most of that money should be invested in a money-market account at a higher average rate of return and which investment would represent only a moderate risk. What should the trustee do?

Analysis: A trustee has no power to invest money which was entrusted to him *for a specific purpose.* Thus, since the $340,000.00 (and more, at the outset of the trust) was specifically designated as a source for repayment of the note, it may *not* be invested in an at-risk investment. The remaining $60,000.00 is probably needed for normal trust administration. The trustee is justified in retaining all of the funds in interest-bearing, fully insured

bank accounts. If the trustee reasonably
believes that a portion of the $60,000
could be invested, his discretion would
likely be upheld if later challenged.

A trustee may hold a portion of the trust funds in
the form of cash or in a non-interest-bearing financial
account to the extent reasonably necessary to enable
an orderly administration of the trust. Probate Code
Section 16225(e). However, the balance of trust funds,
if not otherwise lawfully invested, must be deposited
in: (1) an insured account in a financial institution; or,
(2) if and to the extent the account is collateralized,
an account in a bank, an insured savings & loan
association or an insured credit union. Probate Code
Section 16225(a). If the funds on deposit exceed the
maximum insured or collateralized, the court may
authorize the deposit. Probate Code Section 16225(d).

More generally, a trustee has a legal duty to use
reasonable care to make trust property "productive"
[*In re Armstrong* (1886) 69 Cal. 239], and to keep trust
funds invested in some reasonable manner [*City of
Atascadero v. Merrill Lynch...* (1998) 68 Cal.App.4th
445]. Any unreasonable delay in investing money of
the trust constitutes a breach of trust. *Uzyel v. Kadisha*
(2010) 188 Cal.App. 4th 866; Probate Code Section
16042. Damages for a failure to invest money timely
and reasonably is a trustee liability for interest at the
legal rate. *In re Prior's Estate* (1952) 111 Cal.App.2d
464. On the other hand, one court held that the failure

to invest money which accumulated in a bank account pending distribution would cause the trustee to be liable for the interest which he or she *ought to have received* had the trustee reasonably invested the funds. *In re Whitney's Estate* (1926) 78 Cal.App.638.

The trust itself may absolve the trustee from the duty of investing funds, so long as such provision of the trust is clear and not violative of public policy. *Marsh v. Home Fed. Sav. & Loan Ass'n* (1977) 66 Cal. App.3d 674. Should a trustee retain an investment security in a falling market in the exercise of honest and reasonably prudent judgment, no liability incurs against the trustee for failure to change investments. *Day v. First Trust & Savings Bank of Pasadena* (1941) 47 Cal.App.2d 470. However, the duty to exercise independent judgment in investment decisions is considered to be fundamental and hence *may not be delegated* (i.e., so as to exonerate the trustee from potential liability) by the trustee to any other person or entity, unless the trust provides otherwise. *Martin v. Bank of America...* (1935) 4 Cal.App.2d 431.

Regardless of whether considered speculative and imprudent, a trustee's failure to exercise independent judgment will result in liability of the trustee as to any loss to the trust. *In re Estate of Talbot* (1956) 141 Cal. App.2d 309. California uses the "prudent investor rule" previously described. However, in a determination of whether a trustee has acted prudently in his or her investment decision, certain *factors* come into play:

Jack's Handy Guide To Trusts

◊ the aggregate value of the trust estate;

◊ the nature of other investments of the trust estate; and,

◊ the advisability of diversifying investments in order to insure against unnecessary losses.

Day v. First Trust & Savings Bank of Pasadena (1941) 47 Cal.App.2d 470.

A trustee may not buy and sell on speculation alone. *In re Gartenlaub's Estate* (1921) 185 Cal. 648. A corporate trustee is held to a higher expectation of care, versus an individual trustee, due to its presumed expertise. *Estate of Collins* (1977) 72 Cal.App.3d 663. On the other hand, a trustee is not a *guarantor* of an investment, and once reasonable prudence has been established, the trustee will not be held liable for any loss. *Allin v. Williams* (1893) 97 Cal. 403. Reasonable prudence would normally require a trustee, for example, to investigate the valuation of property to assure that its use as security for a loan to a third party was adequate. *Estate of Collins, above.*

Scenario: Trustee Spencer decided two years ago to invest 1/3 of the trust assets, amounting to $450,000.00 in cash, in A-B Steel Company, traded on the New York Stock exchange. Spencer made this acquisition on behalf of the trust through

Chapter 9
Making Assets Work

a licensed broker. Prior to the purchase, Spencer made no particular inquiry about the company but it turns out that A-B Steel was, in fact, a highly desirable stock. In this regard, Spencer was lucky. The stock rose almost 10% in the first quarter. Thereafter, and for the next seven calendar quarters, Spencer neglected to monitor the stock, except to include its (declining) share price in his annual accountings. The stock broker reports that after the first quarter from date of purchase, Spencer failed to contact the broker despite mailed written quarterly reports of the declining value of A-B Steel and his (the broker's) recommendations to sell. Following his most recent accounting, beneficiary Priscilla filed suit against Spencer alleging breach of fiduciary duty and citing the fact that the value of the A-B Steel shares had fallen 27% from the purchase price. Discovery in the litigation shows several unopened envelopes from the broker among stacks of other mail and receipts.

Analysis: Here, trustee Spencer makes a lucky guess and buys A-B Steel stock, but his luck runs out after one quarter. A trustee is not a guarantor of an investment, but it is also true that a trustee may not buy and sell on speculation alone.

Moreover, a trustee must actually exercise independent judgment in his purchase and sale decisions, and in this case, the stock was purchased *on a whim* without any actual investigation into the risks and potential of the stock. Also, it is incumbent on a trustee to continue to monitor an investment, since that duty is not delegable. He may hire a competent broker to advise and make purchases, but this does not absolve a trustee from periodically and reasonably watching over the actions and decisions of the broker.

In this case, Spencer did even *less* than merely watching over the broker's actions and decisions. Spencer *actively ignored* the broker's attempted letters of advice. The unopened envelopes told the tale and Spencer reluctantly admitted in deposition testimony that his purchase of the stock was essentially, "fire and forget." Spencer would be held personally liable to the trust in damages for the decline in A-B Steel stock prices from shortly after the decline through the date of the judgment, and he would likely be replaced with a new trustee and ordered to reimburse the trust for trustee's fees paid to him during the roughly 2 3/4 year period of his incompetent administration of the trust.

CHAPTER 10
Trusting You

When a person or institution is nominated by a settlor in establishing a trust, that settlor is putting his or her trust, in a real sense, *in that nominee*. In effect, the settlor is saying, "I place my affairs in your hands, to act as my fiduciary, in carrying out the purposes set forth herein as to my trust assets." This real *trust* that the settlor imposes in the nominee trustee is perhaps the center-point of the law of trusts. If a nominee does not wish to bestow upon the trust his time, effort and dedication, then the nomination should be refused so that an alternate nominee which *will* exercise the requisite fiduciary responsibility may undertake the duties as trustee.

In the course of any dispute with the trust, or between beneficiaries of a trust, it is *likewise* important for the beneficiaries to deal with the trust in an honest and straight-forward manner. As described above, violation of a no-contest clause can result in a forfeiture of a beneficiary's interest in a portion or all of the trust. Moreover, a failure by the beneficiary to communicate honestly and fully with his counsel may itself result in other unexpected adverse consequences for the beneficiary. Unreasonable or false claims against the trust will likely result in attorney's fees and costs being expended out of the trust assets, reducing the beneficiary's ultimate share on distribution of trust assets. The failure of a beneficiary or beneficiaries to honestly and fully communicate with their respective legal counsel may lead their counsel down blind alleys which accomplish little and cost the beneficiary substantial attorney's fees and costs. A beneficiary's claims arising from petty motivations such as revenge against the trustee or against other beneficiaries may worsen relations between the respective parties who are family members or otherwise close associates. Thus, in this sense, trust (in the conventional sense of the word) is an important factor in a beneficiary dealing with and instructing his or her attorney in dealing with counsel for the trust.

The main purpose of this *Jack's Handy Guide To Trusts* is to contribute toward a trustee's understanding of trusts and how to, hopefully, administer a trust in such an acceptable manner as *to stay out of court*. Litigation attorneys and forensic accountants are expensive, charging, currently anywhere in the vicinity of $250.00 to $500.00 an hour for their professional services. At those rates, expenses of disputes pile up quickly. Accordingly, trustees (and beneficiaries) of a trust in California may find it useful to be familiar with the precepts of this book, to hire counsel when necessary and appropriate, and to do their best to administer a trust in such a manner as to stay out of court.

Chapter 10
Trusting You

Scenario: Four siblings are all equal beneficiaries of a trust, with the right to receive early distributions, in the form of non-interest bearing loans, in the reasonable discretion of the trustee, and a right to equal distribution of trust assets ten years after the death of the settlor. Five years have passed since the settlor's death and various and differing loans and so-called "advances" from the trust have been made to each beneficiary. The beneficiaries learn of facts which cause them to consult with counsel about a potential breach of trust by the trustee. The beneficiaries each sign a "conflict waiver" which recognizes an "actual or potential conflict of interest" between the beneficiaries and waives that conflict in order to hire one lawyer, Mr. Smithers, between the four beneficiaries. They hire Smithers to enforce or settle their potential claim against the trustee for breach of trust, to have a new trustee appointed or to terminate the trust. The beneficiaries' allegations of breach of trust include the trustee's purported failure to marshal assets of the trust, failure to properly invest assets, use of trust property for purposes not benefiting the trust and failure to properly account. Moreover, the beneficiaries are considering a claim against the trustee personally for resulting damages incurred by the trust. In addition, the beneficiaries all want a new trustee to be appointed or alternatively for the trust to be terminated and for the remaining assets to be immediately, upon Order of the court, distributed. The trustee, in turn, employs counsel on behalf of the trust.

After months of informal discovery, forensic accountings and correspondence between counsel resulting in a progression of more accurate trust accountings, and after the associated considerable expense to the beneficiaries and to the trust, the beneficiaries secretly decide among themselves to lie to their own attorney, Smithers. They decide to instruct Smithers that they now want the trust to be terminated and for the Court to order an equal division of the remaining trust assets, *regardless* of what assets of the trust have been previously loaned or otherwise advanced to each of them. Their *true undisclosed* intent, however, is that after the trust is terminated and the remaining trust assets are distributed equally between them without regard to prior distributions, they will then, among themselves, informally decide how to *re-distribute* such awards so that each of the beneficiaries will have received equal distributions over the life of the trust since the settlor's death. Their motivation in this deception is to save attorney's fees and costs by simplifying the accounting issues as to what each beneficiary has or has not received as a "distribution" or "loan" versus what distributions to each of them respectively from the trust would be considered as general expenses in the normal administration of the trust. They further instruct Smithers to abandon claims against the trustee for any breach of duty and push for a termination of the trust.

Analysis: In this nightmare scenario, counsel for the beneficiaries, protected by the conflict waiver, would be well-advised to promptly obtain a *new* conflict waiver which points out that the conflict of interest between the beneficiaries is no longer merely a "potential" conflict of interest, but has now ripened into an *actual* conflict of interest. If, after taking into account loans repayable to the trust, beneficiary "A" has received significantly more in prior distributions from the trust than beneficiaries B, C and D, and all beneficiaries will divide up the remaining assets *equally*, without regard to the prior distribution, then beneficiary A will eventually receive *significantly more money or assets* than the remaining beneficiaries. For an attorney to represent all of the beneficiaries under these circumstances constitutes an *actual* conflict of interest.

Assuming that a new and improved conflict waiver is drafted and signed by all of the beneficiaries, Smithers could proceed to effectuate his clients' instructions, after consulting with all of them to explain, in person and in detail, the actual disparate result of the beneficiaries' instruction. As mentioned, however, in this scenario the clients have a secret intent among themselves to *redistribute*, after the ensuing court proceeding, the assets among themselves in accordance with their own subjective reconstruction of the respective overall distributions and entitlements. If this secret plan is *revealed* to Smithers, the solution is simple: it would *never* be advisable or permissible for beneficiaries to intention-ally deceive the trust or the court or even their own counsel in this manner. Accordingly, the secret plan would be nixed by Smithers and the legitimate alternatives would be discussed.

Chapter 10
Trusting You

However, if the beneficiaries' secret redistribution plan were *not* revealed to their counsel, Smithers, then at some point in the court proceeding, each beneficiary would be asked under penalty of perjury if they wished to receive an equal share of the remaining trust assets *regardless* of what he or she had previously received or owed back from loans or other distributions and regardless of what the other three beneficiaries have previously received in loans or other distributions. The answer of each beneficiary, assuming they stick with their ignominious plan of deception, would be knowingly false and would, accordingly, constitute perjury. Their sworn testimony would be false because they actually intended to deceive the Court into making such an Order whereas their real plan was to thereafter make their own extrajudicial redistribution of the distributed trust assets. After such (perjurious) testimony, the Court would then (assuming that the plan was accepted by the Court) Order that the remaining trust assets be divided equally regardless of prior loans or other distributions. The money would eventually be paid, by the trustee, to each beneficiary accordingly.

Jack's Handy Guide To Trusts

Several grim deleterious outcomes become immediately possible:

❖ Creditors of any beneficiary could then *execute upon* that beneficiary's share, regardless of any secret intentions.

❖ A *creditor* for a beneficiary who was receiving less than that sum to which he or she would otherwise have been entitled could file a lawsuit against all of the beneficiaries alleging a *transfer in defraud of creditors*.

❖ A beneficiary could *lose or spend* some or all of his or her resulting distributions, leaving, potentially, little or nothing to be "redistributed" in accordance with their informal discussions.

❖ The beneficiaries could, following the court proceedings, *fail to agree* as to how to redistribute the trust asset awards, leading to even more attorney's fees and litigation costs.

❖ A beneficiary holding *more* of the trust assets than the share to which he or she would otherwise have been lawfully entitled could *simply disavow* the secret agreement, point to the statements made under penalty of perjury in court and *refuse to abide* by the secret, undisclosed agreement relating to redistributing the trust assets after the Court's Order takes effect.

❖ The transfer of money from one beneficiary to another, over the permissible annual exempt gifting amount, could arguably create *unwanted taxable income* to the transferee of such transfer.

❖ Lastly, *perjury* in the course of the court proceedings for an Order to terminate the trust and distribute the trust assets could result in *felony criminal charges* being filed against each of the perjuring beneficiaries.

So, as you can readily see from the above scenario, the idea of one or more beneficiaries deliberately deceiving their counsel to attempt to cut expenses in a complicated accounting and factual dispute matter would be a *really, really, bad, idea.*

CONCLUDING REMARKS

I f you find yourself called upon to be a trustee of a trust, consider the following checklist:

1. Read the trust instrument carefully, cover-to-cover. If there is anything you do not *fully and clearly* understand (and there almost certainly will be), consult with independent legal counsel who is competent in the field of the administration of trusts.

2. In deciding whether to accept the nomination as trustee, consider the work to be done in undertaking the role as trustee, your skills and competency to perform as a trustee, the interests of the beneficiaries, the risks of personal liability inherent in acting as a trustee, your available time and energy to enable you to perform the duties and responsibilities of trustee, and the compensation to be earned as the trustee.

3. Determine how well you will or can work with any co-trustee(s) who are nominated in the trust.

4. Do not take actions under the authority of a trustee of the trust if you do not intend by those acts to accept the nomination as trustee.

5. If you do *accept* the trustee nomination, on behalf of the trust, promptly consult with counsel to assist you in the formalities of the administration of the trust and to continue to advise you on the legal meaning of the trust's provisions as well as application of the statutory and case law which pertains to the trust and to you as trustee. Be sure to reasonably vet the attorney/law firm to assure that he/she/it is/are competent in the field of trust administration law and is/are willing to receive no more than reasonable compensation for the work.

6. Always, *without exception,* be honest and forthright in regularly communicating with the attorney(s) which you hire as trustee on behalf of the trust.

7. To the extent available, and if merited by the assets and liabilities of the trust, consider having the trust purchase

insurance to cover your actions as trustee of the trust for any personal liability for negligent breach of your duties and responsibility as a trustee.

8. Take control over and preserve the trust assets—*i.e.*, get them in a state of title and possession so that you, in your capacity as trustee, have control over them in all respects legally possible, and then protect them.

9. Consider hiring experts on behalf of the trust, such as a trust accountant and a stocks and bonds portfolio manager as appropriate to the complexity and nature of the trust assets and liabilities. Be sure to reasonably vet the experts to assure that they are competent in their fields and are to receive no more than reasonable compensation for their work.

10. Promptly render a statement of assets *and liabilities* at the outset of your trustee status in order to document the *starting point*, so to speak, of the trust assets and liabilities.

11. Except as to any liquid funds (e.g., cash or checking account deposits) required for an orderly administration of the trust assets, make the trust assets which are

capable of earning an income, *actually earn an income* through deposit in one or more fully insured or collateralized account as allowed by law or through otherwise prudent investments.

12. Within reasonable periodic intervals (for example, quarterly), personally review and evaluate the trust books and investments to assure that they remain secure, prudent and productive for the trust assets.

13. Treat the beneficiaries as they are intended to be treated in the trust, which typically is without discriminating unfairly from one beneficiary to the other.

14. Follow the instructions of the trust in all regards, particularly as to providing benefits such as income or principal distributions to one or more beneficiary.

15. Retain copies of all receipts and invoices pertaining to expenses of the administration of the trust and continue to maintain legible and properly organized bookkeeping records and entries of all of your trustee actions.

16. *Never commingle* assets of the trust with assets of your own and fully document

any reimbursements to you for your expenditure of personal funds in the proper administration of the trust.

17. Yourself, or more likely through a competent accountant, render a proper (in full accord with the law) and accurate accounting of trust assets, liabilities, receipts and expenditures (including distributions and loans to beneficiaries) *no less than once per year* or more often if called for by the trust, and transmit a copy of that proper accounting to each beneficiary, including notice advisements to the beneficiaries as called for in the Probate Code.

18. Periodically undertake a careful, personal review of the work of the trust's attorney and of any experts or other consultants which you have employed on behalf of the trust in order to reasonably assure that each of them is and has been doing their respective jobs in a reasonably competent manner. Make adjustments in such engagements as appropriate.

If you find yourself becoming a successor trustee after another trustee has arguably failed to fulfill their responsibilities, seek counsel for the trust immediately and take whatever steps are reasonably necessary to bring the trust administration competently up to date as soon as possible. Inform the beneficiaries of the ongoing rehabilitative efforts you are undertaking and invite their cooperation and input. If you have grounds to believe that the trust's current attorney is *culpable*, make the necessary change and hire new competent counsel to represent the trust. Consider the pros and cons of a lawsuit against the prior trustee (and/or against the prior trust attorney) and make a decision in this regard only after detailed factual and legal consultation with the (new) trust attorney (and with the beneficiaries, as appropriate). Treat both the trust, and the beneficiaries with respect. Attempt to administer the trust in accordance with its trust purpose, and do your best—through diligent and competent work and regular and informative communication with the beneficiaries—to keep the peace and avoid unnecessary controversy.

ADDENDUM

In the law of trust administration, the seminal California Supreme Court decision of *Purdy v. Johnson* (1917) 174 Cal. 521 represents a classic case of *what can go wrong, will go wrong* for a neglectful trustee, and of the potential disastrous personal liability of a trustee which may result. Moreover, since the year of publication of *Jack's Handy Guide To Trusts* is precisely *one century* after the publication date of *Purdy*, it seems only fitting to share *Purdy* with my readers. As it turns out, classic problems just never seem to go away. So, please pay homage with your close attention to the California Supreme Court's officially published Opinion in the matter of *Purdy v. Johnson.*

Addendum

ANITA CHRISTAL PURDY, Appellant, v. ROBERT F. JOHNSON et al., as Trustees Under the Last Will and Testament of ALBERTO TRESCONY, Deceased,Respondents.

S. F. No. 7010.
Supreme Court of California, Department One.
March 7, 1917.

APPEAL from a judgment of the Superior Court of Monterey County, and from an order refusing a new trial. B.V. Sargent, Judge.

The facts are stated in the opinion of the court.

Houghton Houghton, for Appellant.

Daugherty Lacey, for Respondents.

SLOSS, J.

The plaintiff is a granddaughter of Alberto Trescony, who died testate in the year 1892. The defendants, Robert F. Johnson and Julius A. Trescony, were the executors of the will of said Alberto Trescony, and are trustees thereunder. At the close of the administration of the estate, a decree of distribution was made, whereby one-third of the residue of said estate was distributed to the defendants as trustees, in trust to manage and control the same for the use and benefit of Anita Christal (now Anita Christal Purdy), the plaintiff herein, and Leo Christal, her brother, until they should respectively reach the age of thirty years, at which time or times the trustees were to pay over to said Anita Christal or Leo Christal, or both, their respective shares of the trust property, if, in the judgment of the trustees, said beneficiaries should "possess such habits of industry, prudence, and economy as to render it suitable and proper and expedient that she or he shall have the control and management of her or of his property." Thereafter, there was a proceeding in partition which resulted in the setting apart to the defendant trustees of certain parcels of land in severalty in lieu of the one-third interest theretofore distributed to them.

The complaint herein, filed in November, 1911, is in two counts. The first alleges that the plaintiff has arrived at the age of thirty years, and that the defendants have informed her that, in their judgment, she possesses the necessary habits and qualifications to entitle her to her share of the trust property, but that the defendants, notwithstanding her demand of a conveyance to her of an undivided one-half interest in said trust estate, refuse to convey the same. The second count is based upon charges of misconduct and impropriety on the part of the defendants in the management of the trust estate. It is alleged that while the defendants were acting as trustees, they filed in the office of the clerk of the county of Monterey, in which the estate of Alberto Trescony had been administered, six accounts of their transactions as trustees. Five of the said accounts were settled by the

Addendum

court, and no appeal had, in any case, been taken from the order settling the account, and the time to appeal therefrom had expired. The sixth account had been set for hearing at the time of the filing of the complaint. It is alleged that the first, second, third, fourth, and fifth accounts were filed and presented to the court for hearing at times when the plaintiff was out of the jurisdiction, and had no notice or knowledge of the presentation of said accounts; and that the trustees had intentionally concealed from her the fact of the filing of said accounts, and of the hearing and settlement thereof. It is charged that in each of said accounts the trustees failed to account for all of the property and moneys received by them for the use and benefit of the plaintiff. They have, it is averred, wrongfully and fraudulently mingled the trust property with their own, and have carelessly and negligently managed said trust, and so carelessly kept the accounts thereof as to deprive plaintiff of a large amount of rents, income, and assets thereof. The complaint specifies a number of instances of alleged misconduct by said trustees, consisting mainly of the renting by them to J. A. Trescony, one of the trustees, of land belonging to the estate at a rental less than that at which similar lands were rented by them to others. It is charged that the other trustee, R.F. Johnson, and his wife, have occupied and used part of the trust property without accounting to the estate therefor; that the trustees failed to credit the trust property with the full amount received from tenants upon leases of portions of the trust property, that they failed to deposit in bank funds of the trust estate, using said funds for their own benefit, and thereby overdrawing their account in bank, and becoming liable for interest for the amount of said overdraft; that they have negligently permitted fences, buildings, and other improvements on the property to become out of repair. As a result of the failure of the trustees to keep proper accounts, the plaintiff has been wrongly charged in the sixth account with a sum of money as due from her to the trustees, whereas, in fact, the trustees are indebted to her in a sum of money exceeding seven thousand dollars.

The prayer of the complaint is that the defendants be required to convey to plaintiff an undivided one-half interest in the trust property; that the orders of the superior court settling the first, second, third, fourth, and fifth accounts of the trustees be set aside; and that the defendants be compelled to account to the plaintiff for all other dealings and transactions with said trust estate.

The answer of the trustees denies all of the alleged misconduct and negligence with the exception of two items inadvertently omitted from the accounts settled by the court; alleges that the plaintiff is indebted to the defendants as trustees in a considerable sum; declares the willingness of the trustees to transfer an undivided one-half interest in the trust estate to the plaintiff upon the settlement of their accounts and payment by plaintiff to them of the sum of, approximately, fourteen thousand dollars, alleged to be due them for advances to her from the trust estate. The answer further denies all of the charges affecting the propriety or conclusiveness of the orders settling the first five accounts filed by the trustees, but declares that, "inasmuch as the plaintiff seems to be dissatisfied with the accounts referred to, in her complaint," the defendants join in plaintiff's prayer, and ask that the orders settling said five accounts be vacated, and that a new account be taken covering the entire period of the duration of the trust, and that upon payment of the amount found to be due by or to the plaintiff, the plaintiff receive from the defendants a conveyance of her interest in the trust property.

The findings of the court were, in the main, in accord with the denials and averments of the answer. It is found that a true accounting between the plaintiff and said trustees shows that the plaintiff is indebted to the trustees in the sum of $8,996.17 for moneys advanced to her by said trustees, which plaintiff refused to pay, and that the protection of the defendants requires that they retain control of the trust estate until the settlement of their accounts and the payment of said balance. All of the charges of concealment, or misrepresentation, of misconduct, and of negligence are negatived. It is found that there are some errors in the accounts filed by the trustees, but these are found to have been inadvertent, merely. There is a further finding "that in all matters

Jack's Handy Guide To Trusts

connected with said trust estate and the management thereof said trustees have acted with the utmost fidelity toward the beneficiaries thereof and have conducted the same with prudence and economy." The court finds that the sum of five hundred dollars per annum is a reasonable amount to be allowed to said trustees as their compensation, this amount having been charged and allowed in the several accounts heretofore presented by the trustees.

The judgment declares that a correct accounting of the trust estate up to January 1, 1909, shows a balance of $8,996.17 due from plaintiff to defendant trustees, and that the defendants recover this sum from plaintiff; that upon payment of said amount to the defendants, the defendants, as such trustees, execute and deliver to plaintiff a conveyance of an undivided one-half interest in the trust estate, but until such payment "said defendants as such trustees may hold and possess all of said trust estate." The plaintiff appeals from this judgment and from an order denying her motion for a new trial.

The appellant attacks these findings and conclusions in almost every conceivable particular. The record is very voluminous, and the appellant's briefs little less so. As it will not be practicable for us to follow counsel minutely into every branch of their exhaustive discussion of the facts and the law, we shall have to content ourselves with a more general survey and review of the situation.

Staying Out of Court

Addendum

The course of the trial was somewhat peculiar. By
their answer the defendants waived any right they
might have had to stand upon the settlement of
their five accounts as a conclusive adjudication of
the matters embraced in the decrees of settlement.
They joined with the plaintiff in asking that every
item involved in their management of the trust estate
be investigated. The answer also admitted certain
inaccuracies in the accounts as rendered. At the
outset of the trial, the plaintiff called the trustees
and examined them and other witnesses regarding a
number of items in the various accounts which had
been presented to the probate court. The trial ran on
in this way for a number of days, when counsel for
the defendants suggested that the case be continued
to enable the trustees to submit the accounts to the
examination of an expert accountant, with a view to
having any irregularities and inaccuracies reconciled
and explained. It was admitted that there were errors
other than those specified in the answer, counsel
saying that "it seems impossible for the court to any
more than guess at what the result should be." After
some discussion, the court granted the continuance,
with a direction that the trustees employ experts and
restate their account. After a lapse of several months,
the hearing was again resumed, and there was
presented to' the court a restatement of the account,
prepared by Mr. Lutgen, an expert accountant. At this
point the plaintiff insisted that the trustees must file
their account and prove its correctness. The course
actually followed, however, was to have the trustees

take the stand without any direct examination on their own behalf, and to subject them to cross-examination by the plaintiff. The ensuing inquiry, involving an examination of a number of witnesses in addition to the trustees, and the production of much documentary evidence, consumed a great length of time.

We think the course pursued was irregular, and that its adoption was the result of a fundamental misapprehension of the nature and extent of the obligation of trustees to account to their beneficiaries —a misapprehension shared by the trial judge with counsel for defendants. As shown by its findings, the court below believed that the trustees had acted throughout in good faith and without any intent to deceive or overreach the plaintiff in any way. We are not disposed to dissent from this view, which we think finds adequate support in the testimony. But, conceding the good faith of the trustees, the fact remains that they had, by their own admission, failed to comply with the obligation which rests upon all trustees to keep full and accurate accounts of the trust funds coming into their hands, and to render an account thereof to their beneficiaries. "Trustees are under an obligation to render to their beneficiaries a full account of all their dealings with the trust fund (3 Pomeroy's Equity Jurisprudence, sec. 1063; 28 Am. Eng. Ency. of Law, 2d ed., p. 1076), and where there has been a negligent failure to keep true accounts, or a refusal to account, all presumptions will be against the trustee upon a settlement. (*Lupton v. White,* 15

Addendum

Ves. Jr. 432, 440, [33 Eng. Reprint, 817]; *Blauvelt v. Ackerman,* 23 N.J. Eq. 495; *Landis v. Scott,* 32 Pa. St. 495.)" (*Bone v. Hayes,* 154 Cal. 759, 766, [99 P. 172].)

The entire trial was conducted upon the erroneous theory that the burden of proof was upon the beneficiary to point out the particulars in which the account was erroneous, and that she was bound to go forward and establish affirmatively the impropriety of the charges and credits which she assailed. Such is not the law.

That the defendants had failed to comply with their duty to keep accurate and detailed accounts is manifest from the facts already recited. In their answer the trustees, after admitting errors amounting to several thousand dollars, allege that the plaintiff is indebted to them in the sum of fourteen thousand dollars. The report of the expert shows an indebtedness of the plaintiff to the trustees of $9,904.95. The court finds that such indebtedness amounted to $8,996.17. These discrepancies, in and of themselves, demonstrate that many errors must have found their way into the accounts as presented.

If we take the statement prepared by the expert as a final account of the executors, the record furnishes no means of ascertaining how the court arrived at its conclusion that the balance due was $8,996.17. There is a mere general finding that the plaintiff is indebted to the defendants in this amount. Upon the new trial, which we shall have to order, the findings should be drawn in such manner as to disclose the particular items allowed and rejected. Even if we accept the ultimate finding as technically sufficient, it must be held the trustees failed to prove an account that would justify the judgment under review. The appellant's attacks upon the various items of the accounts are well founded in at least enough particulars to bring the balance well below the figure found by the court.

A few of the matters dwelt on by the appellant may be mentioned. A one-third interest in certain promissory notes belonging to the estate of Alberto Trescony was distributed to the trustees, and it is claimed that the trustees should have been charged with one-third of the face value of the notes not collected. It was the duty of the trustees to collect these notes, and they were liable for the amount of them with interest, unless they made it appear that the failure to collect the notes was not due to their fault. (*In re Sanderson,* 74 Cal. 199, 203, 204, [15 P. 753].) With respect to two of these notes, that of M. Orradre and that of D. Amestoy, there was no satisfactory showing that the notes could not, with due diligence, have been collected.

The trustees leased a part of the trust lands to J. Parsons, the lease containing a provision for the payment of $458.86 in addition to a proportion of the crop grown. A lease to Charles Parsons called for a payment of $116 in like manner. By the leases the trustees were given a crop mortgage to secure these payments. The cash rentals were not accounted for. The testimony of one of the trustees was that these payments, although described as cash rental, in reality represented a cash advance that had been made to the tenant by the trustees personally. The explanation conflicted with the written lease which the defendants had executed as trustees. Furthermore, the arrangement testified to was in violation of their duty.

They could not use the trust property to secure repayment of advances made by them personally. (Civ. Code, sec. 2229) In so doing they were assuming a position antagonistic to that of their beneficiaries, and any advantage or profit received by them through the transaction is deemed in law to belong to the beneficiaries. (*Western States Life Ins. Co. v. Lockwood,* 166 Cal. 185, [135 P. 496].)

Certain land was leased to Ingram and Sargent at an annual rental of $1,425. The accounts show that only $1,225 was collected for 1894. The appellant claims, and rightly, that the trustees were bound to account for the balance of two hundred dollars, unless they could show some good reason for the failure to collect it. Johnson knew nothing about the subject, and Trescony gave a vague and uncertain explanation which can hardly be termed satisfactory.

Jack's Handy Guide To Trusts

From time to time the trustees advanced money to the beneficiaries for living expenses. In the account prepared by Lutgen the plaintiff was charged with $1,228, claimed to have been advanced to her in the Salinas City Bank, and not charged to her in the original accounts. These charges are attacked as not being supported by vouchers or by the testimony. The objection is supported by the record. The charges were based by the expert solely on memorandum checks or tags found among the papers of the bank. They were not signed by the plaintiff. Such tags do not constitute vouchers showing payment to her. (*Estate of Rose,* 63 Cal. 349.) Furthermore, many of the tags do not purport to be for remittances to the plaintiff, but contain merely the words, "For Remittance. Debit Christal Heirs," "For Check to S. F., Debit Christal. Heirs Estate," "For Ck. D. K. B. Co. Debit Christal Heirs Estate," and the like. The appellants claim that the tags of this class aggregate $700.35. The defendants do not dispute this computation, and we do not feel called upon to make a minute examination of the record to verify the figures. Regarding this charge of $1,228, the respondents say in their brief that the plaintiff was present during the trial and did not take the stand to deny receipt of the amounts specified in the tags. The fault in this argument is that which we have already mentioned as permeating the entire proceeding, viz., that it is assumed that the burden is upon the beneficiary to disprove the correctness of items in the account, whereas, in fact, the burden is upon

the trustees to prove that charges made by them
are proper.

The accounts filed in the probate court, as well
as the restated account of Lutgen, contain charges
against plaintiff for interest, aggregating thousands of
dollars. Early in the history of the trust, the trustees
opened an account with the Salinas City Bank. This
account was almost continually overdrawn, and the
bank charged interest on the overdraft at varying
rates, compounded monthly. If it was necessary to
borrow this money and the terms of the borrowing
were reasonable, the charge was a proper one against
the trust estate. But it appears that during all this
time one of the trustees was collecting money for
the trust estate. This money, or a large part of it, he
would hold without depositing it in bank, and would
pay it out from time to time on behalf of the trust
estate. Obviously, if this money had been deposited
promptly when received, it would have reduced the
overdraft, and consequently the interest charges of
the bank. While trustees are not ordinarily liable
for interest on moneys coming into their hands
unless they have improperly failed to invest them (Civ.
Code, sec. 2261), they are certainly not justified in
borrowing more money than they need, and charging
the trust with interest on the sums so borrowed.
Where they have idle money on hand, it is their
duty to so apply it as to stop unnecessary interest
charges. It is totally impossible to determine from
the record what the proper computation of interest

should be. As is said by respondents themselves, "it is undisputed that these books were kept without any reference to the correctness of the dates of the entry of receipts and expenditures." Upon the new trial, it will be the duty of the trustees to establish these dates, and where they are unable to do so, the computation must be made upon the basis most unfavorable to them.

Numerous other items in the account are attacked by appellant, but we think we have discussed enough of them to show that the judgment appealed from cannot be sustained. The case must be remanded for the taking of a new account in accordance with the established principles of equity. The court may either take the account itself or make a reference for that purpose.

But whichever mode is followed, the account should be stated in accordance with the rules to which we have adverted, i. e., that it is the duty of the trustees to support every item of their account, and that wherever they fail to support the correctness of a charge or a credit by satisfactory evidence, the item must be disallowed.

It is probable that upon any such settlement of the account, these trustees will be compelled to forego repayment of sums which they have properly and in good faith expended for the trust, and that they will be charged as having received money in cases where

Addendum

they have not, in fact, received it, and could not with reasonable diligence have received it. But, if this be the result, it will follow from the failure and neglect of the trustees to perform their duty of keeping full and accurate accounts of their transactions. Their good faith cannot save them from the consequences of this neglect. Whatever doubts arise from their failure to keep proper records or their inability to establish the items of their accounts, must be resolved against them.

We shall not make any disposition at this time of the questions of compensation of trustees and costs, both of which are discussed in the briefs. These matters can be disposed of by the court below upon the new trial, in view of the facts as then developed, and in accordance with equitable principles.

The judgment and the order denying a new trial are reversed.

Shaw, J., and Lawlor, J., concurred.
Hearing in Bank denied.